Roasts

Roasts

Laura Mason

National Trust

First published in the United Kingdom in 2009 as *Good Old-fashioned Roasts*.
This revised edition published in 2019 by
National Trust Books
43 Great Ormond Street
London WC1N 3HZ

An imprint of Pavilion Books Company Ltd

ISBN 9781911358756

A CIP catalogue record for this book is available from the British Library.

25 24 23 22 21 20 19
10 9 8 7 6 5 4 3 2 1

Reproduction Rival Colour Ltd, UK
Printed and bound by Toppan Leefung, China
Photography by Tara Fisher
Home economy by Jane Suthering
Styling by Wei Tang

This book can be ordered direct from the publisher at the website: www.pavilionbooks.com, or try your local bookshop. Also available at National Trust shops or shop.nationaltrust.org.uk.

Reasonable care has been taken to ensure the accuracy of the recipes and instructions in this book. However, any liability for inaccuracies or errors relating to the material contained within the book is expressly excluded to the fullest extent permitted by law.

You may not always achieve the desired results. Oven temperatures vary between different appliances and different equipment may affect the desired outcome. Neither the National Trust, National Trust (Enterprises) Ltd nor Pavilion Books Ltd accept any responsibility or liability for the end results of the recipes featured in this book.

Warning: recipes containing raw eggs are unsuitable for pregnant women or young children.

Contents

Introduction

What is a roast? Much more than a hunk of meat cooked in a certain way. A roast may conjure up images of vast joints of beef turning on spits in front of huge fires, of venison poached from under the gamekeeper's nose, of medieval boards groaning under the weight of peacocks, swans and suckling pigs, of Christmas geese and turkeys, and of convivial Sunday lunch. In short, a roast is an idea of plenty, of feasting (legitimate or otherwise), and of occasion.

And that is what a roast should be. Meat is a resource that is likely to become scarcer – and well-produced meat even more so. We should value it properly for what it is – a food in which months, or possibly years, of an animal's life is concentrated into a package of protein and fat, at once nourishing and delicious, an excuse for a gathering, and provider of meals to come.

Good meat for a roast is expensive and, to some extent, a luxury. This is how it should be – as, too, should be the ability to use meat left over from one meal to make another, equally appealing meal. An element of a long-held idea that British meat is so good that it needs no 'messing about' still persists, but before the 19th century strong flavours were appreciated, as they are once again. Many of the ideas given here try to capture flavours of the past, using as inspiration

recipes from historic cookery texts that would undoubtedly have found their way into the kitchens of houses now owned by the National Trust. Also included are a few forays into current fashions.

The Idea of the Roast

A roast forms a special part of British eating habits, even if it is not quite the weekly punctuation mark it once was. Changes in taste and lifestyle have influenced how people eat; but a well-chosen piece of meat, carefully cooked, is an opportunity for conviviality, a gathering of family and friends.

Originally, roasting meant cooking by exposing meat to radiant heat in front of an open fire. Even casual inspection of historic cookery books shows that this was considered a very important method for cooking meat (and, to a lesser extent, fish). Foreigners remarked on English skill in roasting. Henri Misson, who visited from France in the late 17th century, described cookshops in London with four spits revolving one above another before a fire, each bearing 'five or six Pieces of Butcher's Meat, Beef, Mutton, Veal, Pork and Lamb'. Customers ordered meat done to their taste, and ate it with salt, mustard, bread rolls and bottles of beer. In 1747, another traveller, the Scandinavian botanist Pehr Kalm, wrote that 'English men understand almost better than any other people the art of properly roasting a joint', although his observation that the art of cooking in England didn't extend much beyond roast beef and plum pudding somewhat undermined the compliment.

Spit-roast meat didn't taste of smoke: it cooked in front of the fire, not over it. Fat dripped into a pan set below, with no possibility of overheating. Trying to re-create the flavour of the past is difficult, but experiments give excellent results: succulent, cleanly flavoured, with crisp coatings. Managing the fire correctly, knowing how to spit a joint so that the weight was evenly distributed around it, and how close to put the meat to the fire were all special skills. As a cook, one had to know how to prepare, or dress, and present all sorts of roasts; as a guest, to be able to carve was a desirable social skill. Leftovers were expected and were part of the domestic economy of large households.

A major difference between then and now is that we cook meat in an oven. Technically, this is baking, but it is now the accepted method for roasting. The change to oven roasting began after the coal-fired kitchen range was invented in the 1790s. Gas and electric ovens followed in the 19th century. To people accustomed to spit-roast meat, the change was significant and not for the better. In an oven, meat effectively fries in the hot fat that drips from it, and escaping juices make the fat spit, splashing it on to the sides of the tin, where it burns. The texture of oven-cooked roasts is also different: closer and drier.

Seasonings and accompaniments for roasts have changed over the centuries, from medieval combinations of spices, through tastes for citrus and anchovies, and rich meaty concoctions, to the 'plain cookery' of the late 19th century; our recent adoption of Mediterranean and Asian flavours is another link in this chain. Some items that have shown remarkable persistence are bread sauce, mustard, apple sauce, sage and onion, and redcurrant jelly, all established in the way that we use them today by the 18th century. We look for potatoes to accompany our roasts, but until the end of that century our ancestors would have expected pudding, perhaps a spherical, breadcrumb-and-flour plum one, or a batter type, still with us as Yorkshire pudding.

Sourcing a Roast

The first rule of good roasting is to buy good meat. The British Isles and Ireland have long been recognised for producing excellent meat, especially beef and mutton, but many factors other than simply 'buying British' come under consideration – flavour, price, animal welfare, place of origin. A roast from a supermarket can produce a reasonable meal, but one from a butcher or sourced directly from a farmer is likely to give something much better. Some suppliers are expensive, but others may be cheaper than supermarkets, and a knowledgeable supplier is likely to be able to tell you more about the animals.

Meat lies at the end of the food chain and represents a concentrated and precious food resource. The idea that it should be cheap is erroneous, and on balance it is better to pay a bit more for something well produced and to eat a bit less.

Intensive systems do not automatically equate with poor animal welfare, but for really good flavour, a traditional slow-growing animal is likely to provide better meat. Animal welfare systems have been the subject of much debate over the past 40 years, and several assurance schemes exist to provide the consumer with some idea of how the food on their plate has been produced. There are various schemes, all voluntary, and each with a slightly different emphasis:

• Assured Food Standards ('Red Tractor') – established by the National Farmers Union, it covers many foodstuffs, including meat production in conventional intensive systems.
• Similar schemes exist in Wales (Farm Assured Welsh Livestock or FAWL), Scotland (Quality Meat Scotland or QMS) and Northern Ireland (Farm Quality Assurance or FQA).
• RSPCA Assured (previously Freedom Food) – dedicated to animal welfare, this is the minimum welfare standard that the National Trust will accept from its tenant farmers and when sourcing meat for its restaurants.
• LEAF (Linking the Environment And Farming) – puts a greater emphasis on environmental responsibility.
• Soil Association – this organic certification relates to production systems, and the (non) use of herbicides, pesticides and medication.

All the schemes have their own assessment criteria, inspection systems and logos. Understanding their exact nature will guide you to some extent when choosing meat and other foods, but even within these there are differences. Given that the producers who join them do so voluntarily, the chances are that they will be interested in well-produced food, but ethics and flavour do not necessarily overlap.

Most domestic animals and birds are from commercial stock bred for specific characteristics. Flavour is rarely top of the list – though leanness, fast growth, small bone structure and esoteric factors such as 'double-muscling' may be. Traditional British breeds of cattle, sheep and pig tend to be smaller, slower growing and have more capacity to gain fat than Continental breeds. Slow growth can provide tastier meat and the distinctive appearance of local breeds adds diversity to the landscape. Some breeds are considered 'rare', and there are several marketing schemes for their meat; while eating something rare may seem odd, increasing demand for their meat helps ensure survival.

In conventional agriculture, maximum growth in minimum time is achieved partly by using specially bred animals. They tend to be reared on commercially produced concentrates made from a range of by-products whose composition depends on price. This applies especially to pigs and poultry, whose flesh can be dull and bland. It is less of an issue with beef, which is at least partially grass fed, and least of all with sheep, who graze pasture, moorland or saltmarsh. Farmers who take an interest in flavour often try to grow at least some of their own grain and other fodder crops for poultry, pigs and cattle. Feeding makes most difference to pigs and poultry, and as a general rule, any animal that has roamed freely will be more interesting on the plate.

Don't forget that meat, especially from cattle and sheep, has a strong link with our treasured landscape. Rainfall, temperature and topography are all well suited to grassland, and quite large areas that are unsuitable for growing crops will sustain cattle and sheep. The landscape includes many areas of distinctive flora, often partially created by grazing animals – cattle grazed on the rich lowland pastures of the Somerset Levels or the sweet grasses of the limestone uplands of West Yorkshire, or mutton from the Lake District fells or the short turf of the South Downs.

The age at which an animal is killed for meat also influences flavour. Cattle breeds traditional to Britain score well for flavour, but take a long time to reach the weight at which they make good beef. Most farmers don't want their stock lounging in field or shed eating expensive food after they have reached the optimum weight, so the majority comes from relatively young animals: lamb will be on the market at 4–5 months old, a pig at 3½–4 months. The BSE epidemic led to restrictions on the age at which beef cattle could be sold for meat. These restrictions have now been lifted but the majority of beef cattle are slaughtered at 22–30 months.

An important factor in the production of good meat is the treatment an animal receives at slaughter time, and how that meat is stored afterwards. Body chemistry means that an animal that is calm and rested when killed produces meat that keeps better, cooks better and tastes better. Keeping is particularly important for beef, lamb, mutton and pork, which are allowed to 'hang' in controlled, cool conditions. This process – also called maturing, aging or conditioning – allows changes in the meat to take place, increasing flavour and tenderness. Sheep and pigs are hung for relatively short periods of time, around 1 week. Beef is generally hung for anything between 10 and 21 days; some specialist butchers offer beef that has been aged for longer, for better flavour, but hanging the carcass occupies valuable space and evaporation means that the meat loses weight, thus increasing the price to the consumer. If you can buy beef aged for 28 days or more, it should be very good.

Because of the time and space needed, and the potential for loss of weight during the hanging or dry-aging process, vacuum-packaging – sometimes called wet-aging – is often used. It is claimed that meat undergoes something akin to the maturing process when vacuum-packed. Meat in vacuum packs is, of course, much easier to handle and store.

Where to Buy Meat

Who is likely to sell good meat for roasting? To some extent, finding a good supplier needs trial and error. When buying from a supermarket, look for premium lines that are sourced from specified areas, breeds, groups of farms, or which are given some kind of special treatment (such as long aging). Read the labels. The price will almost certainly be a premium one as well. The more anonymous the meat is, the less likely it is to have been raised and treated with care.

Some of the best meat producers work on a very small scale. One way to source good meat is to get it directly from the farmer who produced it. This has become easier with online retailing. At the same time, local producer groups, farm shops, farmers' markets and food and drink festivals have educated consumers about some aspects of meat production, and have also allowed them to ask, and sometimes to see, how the animals are reared. Through these sources you may also be introduced to suppliers of all sorts of other food.

Alternatively, try to find a butcher you trust, and then cultivate him or her. The Q Guild is an organisation of butchers whose members are committed to excellence. Good butchers will be able to provide much more than a slice of rump steak and a couple of chops.

They should be able to prepare a joint neatly, deboning it if asked (then giving the bones to you along with the meat, of course); do any trimming and tying as necessary; and be able to provide extra beef or pork fat should the meat require it. They should stock breast of lamb and brisket for inexpensive weekday roasts. And they should have some knowledge of the food chain that has produced their meat. Most take great pride in the quality of the meat they sell, and specialise in meat from particular animal breeds or areas. Some have a close working relationship with the farmers who raise the meat, or they 'finish' sheep and cattle themselves, grazing them until they reach their specifications.

Many butchers and farmers' markets sell ready-prepared game, which is available fresh in season (see page 152–187) or frozen at other times of year. Some specialist game dealers send items by post or courier, and for really unusual items such as snipe, woodcock or certain species of deer, your best bet is to look online.

General Information on Cuts of Meat

When you have found a supplier, what should you buy? With a very few exceptions (such as a small rack of lamb), it is a waste of time to roast any piece of meat weighing less than 1kg (2¼lb).

If the roast is just for two, then there will be leftovers, and there are plenty of dishes to make with those. As a very basic rule of thumb, allow about 125g (4½oz) per person for meat off the bone and 250g (9oz) per person for meat on the bone, but don't be too exact about this, especially if the meat is for an occasion when a really handsome piece will make the party extra-special, or if you want some leftovers for other dishes.

The most sought-after roasts are what are known as 'prime cuts', which have a large proportion of tender lean meat and little, or relatively little, connective tissue. They come mostly from the hindquarters of animals. There is a limited supply and a lot of demand, so they are expensive. Secondary cuts, such as shoulder of pork or shoulder of lamb or mutton, are quite fatty with complex muscle structure and more connective tissue; these still make good roasts, but they don't carve as elegantly. Beef brisket and breast of veal, lamb or mutton are well flavoured; they have a layered structure that can make them chewy, but still make good family meals. Belly pork is more tender and is enjoying a revival of interest. In general terms, when buying fresh meat that is cut to order, look at the colour of the meat and the texture of the fat, and avoid meat with a lot of juice running from it, or that has an unpleasant smell.

Bones in meat help to conduct heat, so may shorten cooking times a little. They also add flavour, especially to gravy, and are very useful for making stock (see page 20–21). Joints on the bone can look impressive when the meat comes to the table. On the other hand, they make carving more complex, especially in joints such as shoulder of lamb. Joints such as rack of lamb and loin of pork should be chined – that is, part of the backbone removed – making them easier to carve. Most joints can be boned and rolled by the butcher on request (if you don't feel equal to the task), leaving a cavity suitable for stuffing. Take the bones home for the stockpot.

Fatty meat has been considered a public enemy by nutritionists for more than 50 years, and eating too much fat is certainly not a good idea. But leanness can be overdone too. A roasting joint needs fat; it is fat that gives much of the flavour to meat, and prevents it becoming dry during cooking. Some will be present in layers on the outside of the piece, or between individual muscles; 'marbling' will be visible as streaks and flecks of fat in the lean meat, especially in beef. If fat worries you, remember that some of it will cook out of the meat during roasting and can be skimmed off the juices and then discarded. Visible fat can be cut off your own portion, but don't expect everyone to follow your example.

Meat often arrives vacuum-packed, especially if it has come from a farmers' market or been sent by post. This does produce an odd smell on opening – one that I would describe as dank and vaguely seaweedy. This can be minimised by opening the pack 1–2 hours before use. Discard any accumulated liquid, pat the meat dry with kitchen paper, put it on a plate and cover loosely with foil or a cloth, then leave it to breathe.

With all meat, take special notice of the 'use-by' date if there is one, and keep meat in the refrigerator or freezer as appropriate. Vacuum-packed meat can be frozen to extend its keeping time. Meat will keep well for relatively long periods of time in a deep freeze at a temperature of -18°C (0°F). It is important that frozen meat is properly thawed before cooking. Most pieces will thaw overnight at cool room temperature, although if the joint is very large, or the weather very cold, more time may be necessary. The process can be hastened a little by putting the meat in cold water (never warm) or with appropriate use of a microwave. Put the meat in a container large enough to catch the 'drip' – liquid produced as the meat thaws. Discard this and dry the surface of the meat before starting to cook.

Poultry and Game

Most poultry and game birds arrive swaddled in clingfilm. Remove the packaging as soon as possible and pluck out any extraneous feathers. Avoid washing – splashing water from washing raw meat and poultry under a tap may spread bacteria around the kitchen and increase your risk of food poisoning. With game birds, the packaging makes it difficult to ascertain how cleanly they have been shot and how old they are – only young birds are suitable for roasting. The packaging also means you cannot smell them to tell how 'high' they are (see page 155). Try to find a butcher or game dealer who can supply good-quality birds.

Roasting Equipment

A sturdy tin, of the heaviest gauge metal you can afford, is essential if you plan to roast meat regularly. Tins come in a range of sizes, from small chop roasters to ones that will hold a medium-sized turkey. Use a tin just large enough to hold the joint comfortably, with a little space around it to allow for basting. If the tin is too large, the cooking juices will dry out and burn. A range of materials is also available: anodised aluminium is a good option if heavy steel is too expensive. A light, thin metal tin will do the job of containing the meat in the oven, but it will warp sooner or later – usually the moment you put it over heat to start making gravy. Once a tin has warped, the cooking juices will pool at one end and dry up and burn at the other, and it won't be much use. The oval, enamelled, lidded 'self-basting' tins, which everyone's granny has somewhere in the back of a kitchen cupboard, are solid and big enough for most purposes. For chickens, and for slow-roasting and pot-roasting boned and rolled meat, a deep cast-iron pot with a lid is useful.

It is also useful to have a rack that fits inside a large tin, especially if you intend to roast ducks or geese. A two-pronged fork helps when manipulating hot roasts. A carving fork is fine for this.

Kitchen string, a few skewers and foil are necessities. You may also want to buy a larding needle and a trussing needle (see opposite), and perhaps a meat thermometer and a device for aiding removal of fat from gravy. A nice serving platter or a traditional meat plate look good at the table, but I find a board the best thing to carve on. A carving knife and fork are essentials. The knife must be sharp, so you will need something to sharpen it with – a patent knife sharpener, a steel or a whetstone.

Preparing a Roast

Roasting has a specialist vocabulary and associated techniques, which can add finesse to the results.

Barding and Larding

Very lean roasts benefit from extra fat added before cooking. The easier method is barding, which means covering the surface of the meat with thin slices of fat: bacon draped over the turkey breast is a good example. Bacon for barding needs to be unsmoked, streaked with fat and thinly cut. Pancetta is an option, particularly for small, quickly cooked items such as game birds. Slabs of beef or pork fat can be cut into thin sheets and used to encase lean cuts, or cut into strips and arranged over the meat in a crisscross pattern. The fat will need to be tied onto the meat with string before cooking.

Larding involves inserting slivers of fat, or lardons, into the meat at regular intervals. These melt during cooking and baste the meat from the inside. Pork back-fat cut into narrow strips is the usual choice, but streaky bacon can also be used. A joint can be larded by making incisions with a knife and inserting strips of fat into these (just as sprigs of rosemary and slivers of garlic are inserted into a leg of lamb), but a larding needle will give a better result. This has a hinged flap at the blunt end, which grasps one end of the fat so that it can be drawn into the meat and out of the other side.

If using a larding needle, remember that it is sharp. Some effort may be needed to draw the needle and fat through the meat. The needle may suddenly detach from the fat strip when this is achieved. Push the needle away from you, and don't let children stand near the work surface when you are larding meat. Larding can also be used for adding flavour. Roll the lardons in ground spices or finely chopped herbs to carry flavour into the meat.

Trussing

Trussing isn't really necessary with oven roasting. The vestiges of this once quite complex skill can be seen in the elastic bands put round poultry. In the past, skewers or string were the norm. Trussing keeps meat, especially poultry and game birds, in a neat and tidy shape during cooking, drawing the wings and legs of the bird close to the body. I find that the legs cook more slowly than the breasts of trussed birds, and prefer to remove any strings towards the end of cooking. Discard elastic bands before starting to cook. Skewers and trussing needles are sharp and sometimes difficult to draw through the meat – so take care and keep children out of the way.

Marinating

A marinade can be as simple as a little olive oil and lemon juice with a couple of thyme sprigs, in which the meat is left for 1–2 hours, or an elaborate mixture of wine, herbs and vegetables, in which the meat soaks for several days. With a few exceptions, very liquid marinades are probably not a good idea for roasting joints, because they leave the meat soggy, but rubbing the surface with flavourings such as ground spices can be effective. It is sometimes claimed that marinades with acid ingredients help to tenderise meat. The effect is fairly superficial, but they do add flavour, and some marinades help to extend the shelf life of uncooked meat by a couple of days – useful in the past, before refrigeration.

Stuffing

Boned joints, poultry and game give the cook the opportunity to add a layer of stuffing. It is a technique that was fully exploited in previous centuries. Stuffing can add flavours and fat, provide contrasts in taste and colour, and make a roast go further. Old-fashioned stuffing recipes tend to be quite dense and heavy, and this was deliberate. A texture similar to that of the cooked meat was the aim, so that the two would cut neatly together. Stuffing had the effect of moistening the inside of a joint, the slowly melting internal fat spreading gradually and evenly through meat turning on a spit – an effect mostly lost

in oven roasting. Several mixtures are given here, mostly relatively light and principally for flavouring. Bread-based stuffings should use stale bread – if it is fresh, partially dry it in a low oven. For a light-textured stuffing, tear the bread into small pieces rather than reducing it to fine crumbs, and bind with a little melted butter and stock or milk. For a traditional, dense texture, add beef suet (about a quarter of the weight of this to the weight of bread) and bind with 1–2 eggs. Always calculate the cooking time to include the weight of the stuffing. Alternatively, cook the stuffing separately, baked in a dish, or made into cakes or balls and fried.

Basting

Basting means moistening the meat as it cooks – usually by spooning over the juices and fat rendered during cooking, or extra butter, wine or other liquid. The general idea is to help keep the meat moist by returning to it some of the fat that cooks out during roasting and to add flavour. It is less necessary with oven roasting than it was with spit-roasting, but most meat will benefit from occasional basting. Basting is particularly useful for poultry and game birds, as it helps to develop a crisp and delicious finish to the skin.

Dredging and Frothing

These are methods for finishing a joint to give it a crisp surface. Dredging means adding a coating, usually of breadcrumbs (with or without flavourings), during the final stages of cooking. Frothing means dusting plain flour over the meat a few minutes before the end of roasting. If done with a light hand, the veil of flour effectively fries in the fat on the surface of the meat, literally frothing in the process; this also helps give a crisp, tasty finish to the skin. Too much flour won't cook, and gives what Eliza Acton, writing in the mid-19th century, described as 'an objectionable raw taste'. Sometimes flour is rubbed over a joint at the start of roasting to help the fat crisp.

Pot Roasting

One more step removed from true roasting, this is a method for cooking in a covered container in which the meat fits closely, with flavouring vegetables and aromatics plus a little liquid over gentle heat – braising, in other words. It is useful for meat such as shoulder of venison, which tends to be dry and tough otherwise.

Resting

Meat cooked at a high temperature, or fast roasted, benefits from 'resting' after cooking. This means leaving it on a warmed serving platter, preferably covered, in a warm place (next to the cooker, or in the grill compartment) for about 20 minutes, or longer with large pieces of meat. It is especially recommended for beef. The texture of the meat evens out, making it better to eat. It also gives the cook oven space for Yorkshire puddings or to finish browning roast potatoes, and time for making gravy or sauces, or cooking vegetables at the last minute.

Ovens, Temperatures and Time

Getting to know your oven is important for producing a perfect roast. The quirks of individual ovens make it difficult to predict exact cooking times and temperatures. The all-round 'soaking' heat of Agas and similar stoves makes them very good for slow, even, thorough cooking. Electric ovens are generally even in temperature throughout, especially fan-assisted ones. Gas ovens can be blazing hot at the top and cooler at the bottom, meaning that items must be moved around on the shelves during cooking. If you lack confidence with a new oven, begin with something good-natured and relatively simple – a piece of slow-roast pork, or a boned shoulder of lamb – and eat it with new potatoes. There is no point getting hot and bothered over a huge and expensive sirloin of beef, Yorkshire pudding and roast potatoes.

As a rule, beef, lamb, mutton and game may be cooked to any stage between rare and well done, depending on taste, but pork and poultry should always be fully cooked. Prime cuts can be cooked quickly at high temperatures, but lesser ones need longer roasting at lower temperatures. Roasting time for meat is often calculated by allowing a certain amount of time per pound of meat, multiplied by the weight of the joint; this rule of thumb was worked out about 150 years ago when imperial measurements were the norm, and to convert it to metric, remember that 500g is roughly equivalent to 1lb. Times and temperatures given in the sections on individual meats and recipes are guides.

Meat Thermometers

One way to make sure a joint is cooked is to use a meat thermometer. Insert it into a thick part of the roast before it goes in the oven (make sure it's not touching any bones) and check the reading as cooking progresses. Probe thermometers are also available – these cannot be put in the oven, but are used to take a reading of the internal temperature of the meat if it is removed from the oven. Again, avoid any bones when using these, and withdraw the probe fairly slowly.

Gravy

'Gravy,' wrote Alan Davidson in The Oxford Companion to Food, 'in the British Isles and areas culturally influenced by them, is ... well, gravy, a term fully comprehensible to those who use it, but something of a mystery in the rest of the world.' Possibly some of the confusion is due to changes in the way gravy has been made over the centuries, but it has come to mean either a sauce based on the residues left in the roasting tin with the addition of liquid, reduced to concentrate the flavours, or a mixture made with packaged powder and water.

There is a general perception, promoted by the manufacturers of convenience foods, that gravy should be thick, chestnut brown and plentiful. This isn't always possible by the deglazing method given below, but surely it's better to have a small amount of juice with a really concentrated taste of the meat, than a lot of starch-thickened mixture without much flavour?

Most joints produce a certain amount of juice as they cook. Some of this usually browns on the base of the tin, producing delicious flavours – a process known to chemists as the Maillard reaction. These juices can be used to make excellent gravy.

The general method is this: remove the meat to a serving platter, then pour any fat and liquid from the roasting tin into a bowl. The tin will have patches of slightly sticky, well-browned juices on the base and round the edges. Take a little meat stock (or water from cooking vegetables if the former is not available, or even plain water) and pour into the tin. Use a wooden spoon to scrape all the browned patches into the liquid; you may need to put the pan over a low heat. This process is known as deglazing. Once all the residues have been incorporated into the liquid, add it to the bowl of cooking juices. Skim off any fat, and use the liquid to make the gravy. Wine, cider or brandy can also be used to deglaze, but need to be cooked for a while to mellow the alcohol flavour. Bought stocks can be used, although they may not be as good as a well-produced home-made stock.

Carving

Carving is not about simply cutting hunks off a joint. A good carver can make the meat go further, cut it so that it is more tender to eat, and ensure there are leftovers for another dish. Carving divides the meat, helps everyone to similar portions, or to the size of portion they want, retrieves and divides stuffing from the roast, and shares out limited amounts of desirable pieces – the well-roasted outside, the fat that is considered to taste the best, and the most desirable portions of lean meat.

Much of the ceremonial aspect of carving has been lost, which seems a little sad. After all, the meat on the platter probably represents quite an investment for the household in both time and money, as well as a treat for all those who are about to share it, so why not have a bit of ceremony?

Invest in a good carving knife and fork. The former should have a long, fairly narrow blade with a slightly flexible tip for cutting round bones, and be capable of taking a good edge. The latter will have two long tines, and should have a guard that can be raised to stop the knife blade slipping back up towards your hand. The fork is used for steadying the joint (try not to stab it deeply and make puncture marks); the knife, if properly sharp, will do most of the work.

When carving, bear in mind the direction of the grain of the meat (the muscle fibres) and, as much as possible, cut across it. Joints without bone, such as beef fillet or topside, are simple to carve, as are any joints that have been boned and rolled. With these, it is simply a case of slicing through the meat as if cutting through a Swiss roll (but in much thinner slices – chunky slices of roast are not especially pleasant to eat).

Leftovers

Faced with a leftover joint, one could just eat cold meat, but that is not always the point. For interest, the sake of appearance or for another hot meal, cooks need to be able to use the leftovers of a roast for another dish. A piece of meat is an investment and one should get the best out of it.

Leftovers need care and attention to make them good, just like any other cooking. The cook has to know how to overcome problems such as the potential dryness of cooked meat, diminution of flavour, and a strong chance that someone will have polished off all the gravy. Should there be gravy left, it is sometimes suggested that thin slices of meat can be carved and reheated in it for another 'roast', but this is not satisfactory: the flavour of the meat is never quite as nice, the texture hardens, and the taste is faintly institutional. If a latecomer to the meal insists on a plate of meat and gravy, then fine, but do make sure it is really hot before they eat it. Meat and sauces are favourite homes for food poisoning organisms – and that also goes for dishes made with cooked meat, like shepherd's pie. If leftover dishes are supposed to be hot, they should always be thoroughly hot.

A half-used roast destined for leftovers should be allowed to cool, then covered and stored in the refrigerator. Use the meat within a couple of days, either cold or by converting it to other dishes. For cold meat – in sandwiches or with salad – carve the meat neatly into thin slices. Irregularly shaped pieces can go into dishes where the meat is cut into chunks or minced; trim them of fat and gristle first (those can go in the stockpot). If you can't use cold meat within a short space of time, then wrap it and put it in the freezer. Gravy, too, should be refrigerated and used up within a couple of days, or frozen.

Bones and Stock

Stock is useful for adding to gravy, sauces, soups and many other dishes. If a roast contained bones, use them to make stock (the bones can be frozen if you can't do this straight away). Use a pot into which the bones fit neatly; I use either a two-handled stainless steel pan with a capacity of about 4 litres (7 pints), adequate for a chicken or bones from small to average-sized joints, or a large slow cooker. You will get more flavour if you break or chop the bones, though this may be difficult with stronger ones. Remove any garlic and strong herbs, such as rosemary or sage, lemon, and the remains of any stuffing. Add any scraps of cooked meat too small or dried out to be useful, skin or gristle from the leftover meat, juice or jelly accumulated under the roast, and leftover gravy for which you have no other purpose. Bones left on plates (for instance, from a chicken) are OK to add, as bacteria will not survive the lengthy cooking. Also add fresh flavourings, such as ½ onion (leave the papery skin on); 1 scrubbed carrot, cut into chunks; the green part of 1 leek, well washed; a little celery; 1 tomato; 1 bay leaf; some parsley stalks; a few black peppercorns; and a couple of fresh thyme sprigs.

Don't mix bones from different animal species (except veal or pork bones, which have more neutral flavours and mix well with any others) and don't add salt. Cover with water, put the lid on the pan and bring to the boil. Turn the heat as low as possible and simmer very gently for about 2 hours, checking occasionally. Add boiling water if it seems to be evaporating fast. If you can, put the pan in a low oven, or use a slow cooker, and the stock will be better.

At the end of cooking, strain the stock, discarding the debris. Flavour can be concentrated by fast boiling to reduce the stock. When you feel it's strong enough, allow to cool, then cover and refrigerate. Remove any fat. Stock is best used within 24 hours of making it in summer, or 48 hours in winter. Alternatively, freeze it in convenient amounts for later use, such as in the gravy of the next appropriate roast.

Beef & Veal

Beef has long stood for all things good about food in England, excellent in quality and abundant in supply. To celebrate extraordinary events, whole oxen were roasted, as on the ice of the Thames during the Frost Fairs of the 17th and 18th centuries. On a domestic scale, a roast sirloin or rump of beef was considered the best of food. Privileged aristocrats and their French cooks had game and fancy dishes – but plain beef was the natural food of the upstanding Englishman.

The motif of roast beef appears again and again, in cartoons, prints, in the kitchen scenes depicted in recipe books, in menus real and imagined. Henri Misson in 1719 said of the English that 'two Dishes are their Dinners; a Pudding for instance, and a Piece of Roast Beef'. Later that century, the Norfolk parson James Woodforde was serving the same combination to his tenants for Christmas dinner. Roast beef and Yorkshire pudding is still an ideal Sunday lunch. The pudding might once have been a plum pudding, and now it's always Yorkshire – but the beef remains.

Before railways, the demand for beef was fed by cattle from Scotland, northern England and Wales, driven on foot to fatten in richer southern pastures, sold through the cattle fairs, such as Manningtree, and eventually reaching London. Further back than that, oxen were also important as draught animals, fattened for food only when pensioned off. Beef must have been deeper in flavour (and possibly tougher) than we are now accustomed to. It also appears to have been fatter, judging from some of the 18th-century depictions. During this century, agricultural improvers concentrated on selective breeding for meat or milk, producing beasts of great size. This was the genesis of 'traditional' British breeds that are still valued as meat animals – Beef Shorthorns, Herefords, Aberdeen Angus and others.

In the 19th century, beef – and meat generally – was given extra importance by the infant science of nutrition. Protein was emphasised, and for a while it was thought that all the 'goodness' of beef could be extracted in bouillon and beef tea. The idea was given a commercial push by manufacturers who reduced beef stock by boiling it to a pasty substance, which was packaged in tins – the origin of beef extract (still with us as Oxo and Bovril) and gravy mixes.

Traditional breeds remained the norm well into the 20th century. Many areas of the UK were recognised as producing excellent grass-fed beef – lowland Scotland, much of northern England

and Northern Ireland, less hilly parts of Wales and the Welsh borders, parts of Sussex and Devon. These animals take a long time to reach the optimum weight for meat and are short in the back, so have relatively less of the prime meat used for roasts and steaks than continental breeds introduced in the 1960s. This was a disadvantage when tastes began to change in the late 1960s and nutritionists cautioned against large amounts of red meat and particularly its associated saturated fat. Beef also became more expensive and the BSE epidemic damaged the image of British beef.

Eliza Acton's observation in 1855 that ribs, sirloin and rump were the proper joints of beef for roasting still holds good. These all come from the back of the animal. Sirloin (from the French *sur*, meaning over or upon the loin) has always been prized. It was usually served as a plain roast, although a method known as hashing is described in 18th-century cookery books. When almost roasted, the layer of fat on top of the meat was raised, and the lean meat cut out except around the edges; the meat was finely minced with flavourings and replaced, the fat skewered back down. To us, this seems like an extravagant way of ruining a joint, but it was probably delicious. The long, tender 'undercut', located underneath the

bones of a sirloin and better known to us as fillet steak, was usually left in place and carved with the rest of the joint, but sometimes it was removed, larded or stuffed and roasted or braised, a dish called 'mock hare'.

How the meat of the hindquarter – the rump – was divided in the past is less well known. There are plenty of instructions for roasting a rump or buttock of beef, but it is not clear exactly what was meant. It was obviously a very large piece, weighing up to 7kg (15lb). How closely this coincided with the current definition of rump of beef and adjacent cuts, such as topside, thick flank and silverside, isn't known, but the chump end (which equates to the meat now used for rump steaks) was certainly used as a roast. Two rumps together with the sirloins, still joined together, made a baron of beef – a cut now unavailable, since BSE legislation requires all cattle to be split down the backbone and the spinal cord removed. Roasts from the forequarter have probably always been similar to those used now – rib roasts and sometimes brisket.

Attitudes to veal are more ambivalent than those towards beef. The fact that Britain has plenty of pastureland available all year round for keeping cattle may have encouraged a preference for beef, but veal was eaten as well. Pastureland is not infinite, and some calves (especially in areas that concentrated on cheese-making) have always been culled. Veal used to be a sought-after ingredient, especially in French-influenced haute cuisine. But over the years, and especially in the 20th century, welfare concerns were raised about the conditions in which veal calves were raised, and demand fell.

During the 18th and 19th centuries, veal cuts were close to the ones still used. Flank of veal was sometimes turned into a 'veal goose' by spreading it with sage and onion stuffing, after which it was roasted and served with brown gravy and apple sauce, 'a convenient mode of dressing the flank ...for eaters who do not object to the somewhat coarse savour of the preparation', remarked Eliza Acton rather sniffily when quoting a 'City of London receipt'. It was usual to stuff veal and serve it with sharp sauces to counteract a tendency to dryness and the bland nature of the meat.

Buying Beef and Veal Cuts for Roasting

Roasting beef is as much about cooking good meat by the correct method for the cut, as about recipes. Excellent beef is best bought from a good butcher; the best comes from dedicated beef herds grazing on open pasture and will have been allowed to hang for at least three weeks. The lean should be a good, deep red colour (not bright red) and lightly marbled – flecked with streaks of fat. The visible fat should be creamy-white and crumbly in texture.

Although milk-fed veal at 2½–3 months old is still considered the best, there is an alternative: this is 'rosy', or rosé, veal, a deep pink colour with a light streaking of fat in between the muscles. It comes from older, loose-housed or outdoor-reared calves. Tracking it down takes persistence, and once you find it, you may have to order roasting joints. A butcher who deals with the catering trade, or the internet, are the most likely sources.

What to Buy, and How Much

The British method of butchering beef and veal tends to run across major muscle groups, cutting through fat and bone (rather than dissecting muscles out, which tends to be the practice in continental Europe). In the past, the names for cuts varied quite a lot regionally, although they appear to be fairly standard now. Sirloin is expensive, and if you want a piece from the rear end of the joint with the fillet still in place, you may have to order it: the joint is more profitable when divided into sirloin, fillet and T-bone steaks. Working forwards, the front part of the sirloin is also known as the wing rib, with a good eye of lean meat but no undercut. Attached to this is the forerib, with streaks and layers of fat in the 'tail', getting progressively less lean. These joints respond well to fast roasting at relatively high temperatures. Buy sirloin by weight, and rib joints by number of ribs, although they can be boned and rolled (which makes them easier to carve, but less splendid at the table). A fillet, or a piece of one, will be expensive and is usually used for Beef Wellington (see page 34 for a very special sandwich using this cut). Brisket (boned and rolled) has an excellent flavour, but is highly variable in size and fat content, and tends towards toughness. Be guided by the butcher's opinion, and treat it gently, with long, slow cooking. Working back from the sirloin, the next cut is the rump, now principally used for steaks; behind this, at the top of the hind leg, lies topside, a very lean piece of meat that makes a good slow roast; and next to it the silverside and a muscle known as the pope's eye, also possible roasting joints. These need to be slow roasted or pot roasted.

Veal cuts for roasting include loin (equivalent of the sirloin in beef cattle), the chump end or fillet and topside; towards the head, the best end (equivalent to a beef rib roast) and shoulder; the breast can also be boned and rolled with stuffing. Veal is lean and tends to dry out, so treat it gently and use a slow-roast method with secondary cuts.

Storage and Preparation

The British have traditionally considered that any home-produced roasting beef is full of flavour and far too good to be 'messed around with' – for example, marinated or otherwise flavoured before cooking – and that when cooked appropriately, the meat will also be sufficiently tender. As far as flavourings are concerned, beef fillet (less pronounced in flavour than many cuts) can benefit from short marinating with oil and herbs, and light spicing makes an interesting change with slow-roast cuts. Otherwise, restrict seasonings to salt and pepper, and possibly a little mustard powder mixed with plain flour and rubbed into the fat of a sirloin or rib roast before cooking. Very lean beef, such as topside, benefits from barding with extra fat (see page 15). Veal has a delicate flavour that is easily overpowered by strong seasonings. Good contrasts are light, lemony notes; salted meat such as ham or bacon; the nutty flavours of some fortified wines; and a mild mustard of the Dijon type. Stuffings are a good idea with veal. Because it is from young animals without much fat, veal can be dry. To help prevent this, bard with pork fat or spread a little butter over it before cooking. If you can obtain some veal bones (even in relatively small quantities) and use them to make stock, these will enhance veal gravy and many other dishes.

Times and Temperatures

How 'done' should roast beef be? Some people hate well-done beef; others don't like to see pink in the middle. In the mid-20th century, well-done meat seems to have been the norm, but since the 1980s, chefs and cookery writers have shown a very definite preference for underdone meat generally. If you are intending to use some of the beef cold or for leftovers, it's better if it is kept slightly rare. Very lean cuts of beef, such as topside, are better if they are done on the rare side of medium, because they tend to dry out during prolonged cooking. Really, it's a matter of taste.

There are two basic methods for roasting beef. The first is sometimes known as high-heat or fast roasting. For a fast roast, give the meat 20 minutes at 240°C, 475°F, Gas mark 9, then reduce

the heat to 180°C, 350°F, Gas mark 4 and cook for the following times:

- Beef on the bone: 15 minutes per 500g (rare); 18–20 minutes per 500g (medium); 25 minutes per 500g (well done).
- Boneless beef: 12 minutes per 500g (rare); 13–15 minutes per 500g (medium); 20 minutes per 500g (well done).

The second method is slow roasting. Cook at 150°C, 300°F, Gas mark 2 for the entire time, allowing 20–25 minutes per 500g for rare to medium, and 30–35 minutes per 500g for well-done meat. Cook pot roasts even more slowly, at 140°C, 275°F, Gas mark 1, and up to 60 minutes per 500g.

Veal, because it tends to dryness, needs gentle heat. It should always be well done, but be careful not to overcook. Start it at 190°C, 375°F, Gas mark 5 for 15 minutes, then turn the heat down to 180°C, 350°F, Gas mark 4 and allow 25–30 minutes per 500g.

Roast Beef and Yorkshire Pudding

SERVES 6

a piece of sirloin or rib roast,
    or wing rib or forerib
1 tablespoon plain flour
1 teaspoon mustard powder
salt and pepper
about 300ml (10fl oz)
    beef stock

FOR THE PUDDING
2 eggs, beaten
100g (4oz) plain flour, sifted
a pinch of salt
150ml (5fl oz) milk mixed
    with 150ml (5fl oz) water
beef dripping from the roast

Take the beef out of the refrigerator about 1 hour before you want to start cooking it. Calculate the cooking time by the fast-roasting method (see page 27). Preheat the oven to 240°C, 475°F, Gas mark 9. Season the flour with the mustard powder, salt and pepper, and rub it into the fat. Put the meat, bones downward, into a suitable roasting tin and roast for 15 minutes, then reduce the heat to 180°C, 350°F, Gas mark 4.

While the meat is roasting, prepare the pudding batter. Mix the eggs, flour and salt. Then use a whisk to blend in the milk and water, to make a batter with the consistency of thin cream. Leave to stand.

After the beef has been removed from the oven to rest, turn up the heat to 220°C, 425°F, Gas mark 7. Add 1 generous tablespoon of dripping to the Yorkshire pudding tin and heat it in the oven until smoking hot. Pour in all but about 2 tablespoons of the batter (it should hiss spectacularly if the fat is at the right temperature), then return the pudding to the oven. Cook for about 30 minutes, until it is well browned in patches and light and crisp in texture.

To make the gravy, take the tin the beef was roasted in and spoon off any excess fat. Deglaze with the stock. Let this bubble, and then, off the heat, stir in the remainder of the Yorkshire pudding batter, and keep stirring until the mixture thickens (you may need to heat it gently to achieve this). Add a little more stock if necessary, then taste and adjust the seasoning.

To follow tradition, cut the pudding into squares and eat with gravy before the meat.

Slow Roast Topside

Slow roasting is a good method for lean joints such as topside whose low fat content means they have a tendency to be dry.

SERVES 6

beef topside, 1.5–2kg
   (3½lb–4½lb)
extra beef fat, cut in thin
   slices for barding
   (optional)
salt and pepper
about 150ml (5fl oz)
   beef stock
about 1 tablespoon plain flour

If you wish to bard the topside, arrange the fat in a layer over the meat and tie it on with string. Put the meat in a roasting tin that it fits reasonably well. Put in a low oven, 150°C, 300°F, Gas mark 2 (use the highest shelf in a gas oven) and allow 25 minutes per 500g for rare to medium-rare meat, 30–35 minutes for well done. About two-thirds of the way through cooking, season the meat with salt.

When the meat is cooked to your taste, remove it from the tin to a hot dish. Snip the strings holding the fat in place and discard them and the remains of the fat (the fat should have cooked through, so you may find it crisp and delicious). Keep the meat warm. Pour the cooking juices out of the roasting tin into a bowl, then deglaze the tin with a little stock and add this to the juices. Skim them, returning 2–3 tablespoons of fat to the roasting tin; stir in a little flour and allow it to cook and brown gently. Stir in the juices, plus stock as necessary, to make the gravy; taste and correct the seasoning, then serve.

Pot Roast Brisket of Beef

Brisket is not an elegant joint, but it has an excellent flavour. This recipe is based on 'To stew a Rump, or the fat end of a Brisket of Beef in the French Fashion', recorded by Robert May in The Accomplish't Cook *(1660).*

SERVES 6

2kg (4½lb) piece of
    rolled brisket
1 tablespoon olive oil
a handful of shallots, peeled
1 garlic clove, peeled
    and sliced
1 scant tablespoon plain flour
200ml (7fl oz) red wine
about 150ml (5fl oz) beef
    stock (optional)
1 teaspoon salt

FOR THE MARINADE
2 teaspoons black peppercorns
2 blades of mace
6 cloves
fresh root ginger, about 1cm
    (½in) cube, peeled and
    finely grated
1 generous dessertspoon
    demerara sugar
1 garlic clove, peeled
    and crushed

To prepare the marinade, put the peppercorns, mace and cloves in a mortar and crush roughly. Stir in the ginger, sugar and garlic, then rub the beef with this mixture. Cover and leave overnight in a cool place or in the refrigerator.

To cook the meat, wipe the beef to remove most of the ground spices. Heat the oil in a casserole and cook the shallots and garlic briskly, stirring frequently, until they begin to brown slightly. Remove to a dish, then put the beef in the casserole and brown it all over. Then put the shallots and garlic around the meat, sprinkle over the flour and add the wine. It should cover the base of the casserole to a depth of about 2cm (¾in).

Fit a doubled sheet of greaseproof paper neatly across the top of the casserole, trimming so that it doesn't stick out and burn, then put the lid on over this. Cook very gently for 4 hours; this can be done on the lowest possible heat on top of the stove, or in a low oven at 140°C, 275°F, Gas mark 1. Check occasionally, especially if cooking on top of the stove, and add a little stock if necessary, as the gravy tends to reduce and catch; also, sprinkle the salt over the meat.

When cooked, remove the meat to a serving dish. Pour off the gravy and set it aside for a few minutes, then skim off the fat. You should be left with a glossy, deep-brown, rich-tasting sauce, which can be thinned with a little stock or water if you like. Check the seasoning. Slice the meat thinly, and pass round the gravy and some mashed potatoes (see page 200).

Steak Sandwich

SERVES 4

a piece of fillet steak from the
 'tail' end, weighing about
 500g (1lb 2oz)
2 tablespoons olive oil
100g (4oz) button mushrooms,
 sliced
15g (½oz) dried sliced porcini
 mushrooms (optional),
 soaked in 100ml (3½fl oz)
 warm water for 30 minutes
 – keep the soaking liquid
1 ciabatta loaf
salt

FOR THE MARINADE
4 tablespoons red wine
2 teaspoons balsamic vinegar
1 garlic clove, peeled
 and crushed
1 dessertspoon finely chopped
 parsley
1 bay leaf, shredded
3–4 thyme sprigs, leaves only
3–4 marjoram sprigs, leaves
 only, chopped
2 tablespoons olive oil
freshly ground black pepper

Mix the marinade ingredients and put them into a shallow dish
or bowl. Add the piece of fillet, rubbing well with the mixture,
and leave to marinate, turning from time to time, for a minimum
of 2 hours. It can be left for as long as 24 hours. Preheat the oven
to 230°C, 450°F, Gas mark 8.

Heat the oil in a frying pan or a small, shallow cast-iron
ovenproof dish. Add the sliced button mushrooms and fry
briskly, stirring from time to time, until they begin to brown
slightly at the edges. Stir in the soaked porcini and add their
soaking liquid. If you have used a frying pan, transfer the
mushroom mixture to an ovenproof dish at this point. Lift the
beef out of the marinade, rubbing off any debris, and lay it on
top of the mushrooms. Pour the marinade in underneath. Roast
for 15–20 minutes. The meat should be rare to medium.

Slice the ciabatta in half lengthways and remove some of the
crumb from each half, to leave a hollow into which the meat
will fit. When the meat comes out of the oven, lay it in one side
of the bread and distribute the mushroom mixture over it. The
cooking liquid should have reduced to a few tablespoons (if it
hasn't, reduce it by fast boiling). Pour the liquid over the meat
and mushrooms. Season with a sprinkling of salt. Put on the top
half of the loaf, pressing it down firmly to enclose the filling.
Wrap firmly in foil, clingfilm or greaseproof paper. Put a small
board on top and weight lightly with a couple of books or tins.
Leave for 5–6 hours, then unwrap and cut across in slices at least
1cm (½in) thick.

Roast Veal with Sorrel Purée

A traditional combination lovely for a meal in late spring. Sorrel is not easy to obtain, but it is worth growing it or trying to buy some because it makes a delicious accompaniment for many things besides veal. For sorrel purée the relative amounts of sorrel and cream are fairly flexible.

SERVES 6

a piece of veal for roasting
    (topside, loin or chump),
    about 1.5–2kg (3½lb–4½lb)
30g (1oz) unsalted butter
1 scant teaspoon finely grated
    lemon zest (preferably
    unwaxed)
½ teaspoon black peppercorns,
    coarsely ground
1 fresh bay leaf – discard the
    central spine, and finely
    shred the leaf
salt

FOR THE SORREL PURÉE

15g (½oz) unsalted butter
100g (4oz) sorrel, washed and
    picked over – remove any
    tough stalks
150ml (5fl oz) double cream
salt and pepper

An hour or two before you want to cook the veal, soften the butter and mix in the lemon zest, pepper and bay leaf. Rub this mixture all over the meat and leave it, covered, in a cool place.

For cooking, select a roasting tin or casserole into which the meat will fit neatly, without too much space round the edges. Do not cover. Preheat the oven to 190°C, 375°F, Gas mark 5. Cook for 15–20 minutes, then reduce the heat to 180°C, 350°F, Gas mark 4 and continue to cook, basting with the juices from time to time. Salt lightly towards the end of cooking, and rest for 15 minutes.

Just before serving, make the sorrel purée. Melt the butter in a saucepan. Put in the sorrel, still damp but not wringing wet from washing, then stir over gentle heat until it collapses. The colour will change from a vivid green to a less attractive grey-brown, but don't let this worry you. As soon as it is all cooked, remove from the heat. Pour the cream into a clean pan and bring to the boil. Add the sorrel and cook gently for 2 minutes; add seasoning to taste.

Carve the meat in thin slices and spoon some of the buttery cooking juices over each plate. Serve with new potatoes and the sorrel purée.

Veal with Orange and Verjuice

The original idea for this came from a book first published in France by an author known simply as La Varenne. Translated into English as The French Cook *(1653), it was an important text in the development of cookery techniques. This recipe uses verjuice (the juice of unripe apples or grapes), and it gives a pleasant fruity sourness without being overwhelming. If you can't get verjuice, use a not-too-dry white wine in this recipe.*

SERVES 6

a piece of veal topside, about
 1.5kg (3½lb)
40g (1½oz) unsalted butter,
 softened
salt
about 200ml (7fl oz) stock,
 preferably veal or chicken
about 1 tablespoon plain flour

FOR THE MARINADE

zest of 1 orange (preferably
 unwaxed), in thin strips
zest of ½ lemon (preferably
 unwaxed), in thin strips
6 tablespoons verjuice or wine
freshly ground black pepper

For the marinade, mix the orange and lemon zests with the verjuice and a little freshly ground pepper. Turn the veal in this mixture and leave to marinate for 5–6 hours, or overnight.

When you want to cook the meat, remove it from the marinade and scrape any bits of zest back into the marinade mixture. Preheat the oven to 190°C, 375°F, Gas mark 5.

Spread the butter over the meat, add a little salt, and put the meat in a roasting tin into which it fits reasonably well. Strain in the liquid from the marinade. Cook in the preheated oven for 15 minutes, then reduce the heat to 180°C, 350°F, Gas mark 4 and allow 25–30 minutes per 500g, basting frequently and adding a little stock to the tin if the juices show signs of drying up. About 15 minutes before the end of cooking time, add the zest from the marinade to the roasting tin (do not add it any earlier, or it will burn and blacken).

When the meat is done, remove it to a warmed serving dish and allow to rest. Pour the juices from the tin into a bowl. Deglaze the tin with a little stock, then add this to the juices. Spoon off excess fat, returning about 1 tablespoon of the liquid to the roasting tin, and sprinkle in a little flour. Stir over a low heat until it browns slightly, then stir in the cooking juices to make gravy.

LEFTOVERS

Beef is one of the nicest meats to eat cold. A slice or two, slightly underdone, with a salad of green leaves and some potato salad, is excellent as a lunch or light evening meal for a hot day. It also makes good sandwiches (see below). Several recipes developed for other meats are also suitable for cold beef, including Shepherd's (or Cottage) Pie (see page 63), Hashed Meat (see page 86), rissoles (see page 87) and croquettes (see page 184).

Veal is less interesting when cold – the flavour becomes positively bland and the dryness is accentuated. British cookery has few solutions for what to do with the remains of a roast of veal. It can be used for French Stuffing for turkey (see page 127) and Eliza Acton's Veal Loaf (see page 45).

COLD ROAST BEEF SANDWICHES

SERVES 4

8 slices of bread, lightly buttered
4 dessertspoons mayonnaise
horseradish sauce, to taste
cold roast beef, sliced thinly
salt and pepper
gherkins or preserved cucumbers with dill

Lay out the pieces of bread destined to make the base of the sandwiches. Mix some mayonnaise (about 1 dessertspoon per sandwich, if using slices from a standard loaf) with a little horseradish to taste, and spread it over each slice. Distribute the beef over this, then season lightly, and add a few slices of pickled cucumber to each one. Complete with the remaining slices of bread.

SERVES 4

8 slices of bread, lightly buttered
4 dessertspoons mayonnaise
Dijon mustard, to taste
cold roast beef, sliced thinly
Crisp Fried Browned Onions
    (see page 210)
salt and pepper

Proceed as above, but mix a little mustard into the mayonnaise instead of horseradish, and scatter the onions over the beef.

BUBBLE AND SQUEAK

This can hardly be said to be a recipe: it is more a method for reheating various bits of leftover roast lunch. There are probably as many versions of bubble and squeak as there are people who make it. Originally a dish of fried cold beef, cabbage and potatoes appeared in recipes in the late 19th century (perhaps influenced by Irish colcannon) and other vegetables were sometimes added. In the mid-20th century, it was often served with sliced cold beef.

There are few rules in making bubble and squeak: the ingredients and their proportions depend to some extent on the contents of the larder. Leftover cabbage and mashed potato, fried, remain the two crucial ingredients. Aim for about half and half by volume of the two vegetables. The variety of cabbage may vary, but whatever is used, it must be well drained. Adding fried onions or bits of fried bacon is entirely up to individual taste, as is the medium used for frying. Beef or pork fat left from a roast, or bacon dripping, are all good. Butter burns too easily to work well with a potato-based version. Avoid oil, and fat from lamb or mutton.

Heat a frying pan and add a little fat – just enough to cover the base – and when hot, add the bubble and squeak mixture. Allow this to cook until the underside is nicely browned and crisp, then turn with a spatula. Don't worry if the 'cake' breaks up (one that keeps its shape is worryingly reminiscent of industrially produced versions), but continue to cook gently. Turning the mixture more during cooking evaporates some of the moisture and consolidates the mixture, although you will get a certain amount of the browned crust mixed into it.

Serve on its own, with cold beef, or reheated gravy, or as part of a breakfast fry-up.

BEEF RAGÙ

A reasonable beef ragù (the type of sauce better known in English as Bolognese sauce) can be made with leftover roast beef. It won't be as good as one made with fresh beef, but provided it is made with care and good ingredients, it will be quite acceptable mixed through a bowl of pasta or used to stuff vegetables for baking, such as hollowed-out courgettes.

SERVES 4–6

30g (1oz) unsalted butter
60g (2½oz) unsmoked pancetta or lean bacon, finely chopped
1 medium onion, peeled and finely chopped
1 small carrot, coarsely grated
1 celery stick, finely chopped
2 large mushrooms, finely chopped
2 garlic cloves, peeled and crushed
250g (9oz) cold roast beef, trimmed of fat, gristle and outside bits, and minced
150–200ml (5–7fl oz) red wine
100–150g (4–5oz) passata
1 bay leaf (optional)
a pinch of dried thyme (optional)
a pinch of dried marjoram (optional)
scant 1 teaspoon salt
freshly ground black pepper

Melt the butter in a large frying pan or flameproof casserole and fry the pancetta until the fat is translucent. Add the onion and cook over low heat until it begins to soften. Add the carrot, celery, mushrooms and garlic, and continue to cook, stirring from time to time, until the vegetables begin to soften and brown. Add the beef and stir in well, then pour in the wine and allow it to bubble. Stir in the passata and the herbs, if using, and finally season with the salt and grind in some pepper. Simmer very gently for about 1 hour. Taste and correct the seasoning.

COLD BEEF, HASHED

The standard English method for re-presenting leftover beef (or any other meat) was to make it into a hash – cutting the meat up small, making a sauce to reheat it with, and adding flavourings as taste and imagination dictated. 'There is not any Thing in which the Cook may so much indulge her Fancy as in a Hash; for almost any Thing may be put into it', wrote Martha Bradley in The British Housewife *(1756). This is Alexis Soyer's 'Hashed Beef Another Way', from the mid-19th century, which works well with small amounts of beef to make a dish for one or two people.*

SERVES 2

15g (½oz) unsalted butter
1 tablespoon finely chopped onion
50g (2oz) sliced mushrooms (optional)
75–100g (3–4oz) cold roast beef, cut into
    small thin slices
1 dessertspoon plain flour mixed with
    a little salt and pepper
150ml (5fl oz) beef stock
1–2 pickled gherkins, sliced
some vinegar from the gherkins
salt and pepper
1 teaspoon chopped parsley or tarragon
    (optional)
walnut ketchup, to taste (optional)

Melt the butter in a frying pan. Add the onion and cook briskly, stirring frequently, until lightly browned. Add the mushrooms, if using.

Toss the slices of meat with the seasoned flour, then add them to the onion and turn them in the pan to warm through. Add the stock plus the gherkins and a little of their preserving vinegar (don't overdo this; you can always add a little more towards the end). Bring to a simmer, then taste and add more seasoning if desired. If using the chopped herbs or walnut ketchup, add these at the end as well.

BEEF AND VEGETABLE BROTH

SERVES 4

1 litre (1¾ pints) good beef stock
¼ medium turnip or swede, peeled
1 leek, trimmed
3 celery sticks, trimmed
a few leaves of curly kale
2 large carrots, trimmed and peeled
salt and pepper

Put the stock in a pan (one that will go in the oven is a good idea, or use a slow cooker) and bring to the boil. While it heats, chop all the vegetables finely and add them to the pan. Stir in 1 teaspoon salt. Cover, and when it boils, transfer to a low oven or a slow cooker and leave to cook. It should be ready after about 1½ hours.

The fresher the vegetables, the better the soup will be. Finely chopped celeriac or a tomato, skinned and chopped, are all good additions.

ELIZA ACTON'S VEAL LOAF

Eliza Acton gave this recipe in her book Modern Cookery for Private Families *(first published in 1845) under the name of 'Bordyke veal cake' (Bordyke was the street in Tonbridge where she lived). It works well with the remains of a roast, and it makes a meatloaf like a close-textured, coarse pâté.*

SERVES 6–8

700g (1½lb) cold roast veal, free from bones, fat and gristle
225g (8oz) unsmoked streaky bacon
2 medium eggs, lightly beaten
zest of 1 lemon (preferably unwaxed)
a generous pinch of cayenne pepper
a pinch of grated nutmeg
½ teaspoon ground mace
½ teaspoon salt
unsalted butter, for greasing

Preheat the oven to 180°C, 350°F, Gas mark 4. Mince or chop the veal and bacon together thoroughly. Mix in the eggs, lemon zest and all the seasonings. Grease a round ovenproof dish and pack in the meat mixture. Cover the surface with foil or buttered greaseproof paper. Bake for 1–1¼ hours. Smaller amounts can be packed in individual ramekin dishes, which need about 25 minutes baking.

Eat hot with a light tomato sauce, or cold with salad and new potatoes.

Lamb
& Mutton

Lamb and mutton both refer to the meat of sheep, but – unless you are a shepherd or a butcher – the terminology can be confusing. Alive, a sheep is considered a lamb from birth in the spring until the turn of the year. For the next 12 months, the animal becomes a hogget, and after that it is a sheep.

As meat, lambs may be killed at about 10–12 weeks old for Easter, but most reach the market at between 5 and 12 months (still called lamb, and probably what 19th-century authors referred to as 'grass-fed lamb'). The meat of an animal between one and two years old is known as hogget; with a richer flavour than lamb but just as tender, since it is usually hung for 10–14 days. After its second winter, the meat becomes mutton and will taste more interesting, especially if grazed on some distinctive species-rich grassland or hill pasture. The full flavour develops at around 3 years old, but the best mutton comes from animals 5 or even 6 years old; they are hung for about 3 weeks and, cooked carefully, the meat is beautifully tender. Wethers – castrated rams – were thought to give the best meat, but this is impossible to buy these days.

Mutton seems to have lost favour some time shortly after the end of World War II, and people are just beginning to appreciate its flavour once again. Our ancestors ate a lot of mutton, some of it very fatty and coarse, which is probably why the market for it declined when ample supplies of frozen New Zealand lamb became available. Until the mid-19th century, there was a certain amount of 'house lamb' production, indoor rearing of out-of-season young lambs. These animals, which had pale, tender flesh but not much flavour, were a luxury for Christmas, eaten young.

Lamb, in the sense in which we now understand it, is more seasonal than beef: usually born between January and May in the British Isles. New season's lamb is sought-after for Easter, when the home-bred item will just be coming on to the market (some farmers lamb around Christmas specifically to supply the Easter market). The bulk is available in late spring and early summer, running through to September or October.

Lamb and mutton, when it arrived before the roasting range in kitchens of the past, was, like beef, sometimes regarded as too good to be messed around with. The best mutton was simply roasted, as was young house lamb. Another dish involved hollowing out the lean meat from a partly roasted joint – in this case, from the inside of the leg – then chopping and pounding the meat with flavourings, and stuffing it back in the cavity and returning it to roast. The meat off a shoulder, roasted until almost done, was also sometimes taken off the bone, and the meat cut away from the inside and hashed (from the French, to chop or mince). The bones and outer layer were grilled and served on top of the hash, a dish sometimes called 'Shoulder of Mutton in Epigram'.

We tend to forget that lamb was much anticipated as a meat for the early summer, best with summer vegetables – peas, new potatoes and small turnips. Mint sauce fitted in with this general summer scheme. In the 18th century, cucumber-based dishes were often served with mutton, while the 19th-century preference was for redcurrant jelly or onion sauce. Stuffing was sometimes used with meat from sheep, more to soak up fat than to add it.

British cookery has a persistent thread of serving lamb or mutton with flavours derived from the sea. Laverbread – a type of seaweed – is one example, as is samphire (plainly cooked, and served as a vegetable accompaniment, or cut into short lengths and stirred into the gravy). Fish flavours such as anchovy are also found in many recipes and go surprisingly well with the meat, more so if you can source a piece of saltmarsh-grazed meat. A favourite combination in English cookery books during the 17th and 18th centuries was mutton with oysters – cheap and easily available, oysters were mixed into stuffings, rolled in spice and herb mixtures and used to lard the meat, or added to the sauce. The dish went out of fashion in the second half of the 19th century, with the decline of oyster beds around the British coast.

During the second half of the 20th century, cookery writers began to introduce ideas from the peasant and country kitchens of southern Europe and the Middle East. Strong herb flavours and the use of fruit with lamb or mutton reappeared in English cookery after an absence of about four centuries. The idea of larding a leg of lamb with slivers of garlic and sprigs of rosemary, or concocting a rice and apricot stuffing, come from this interest in Mediterranean traditions.

Buying Lamb and Mutton for Roasting

Butchers often identify where their lamb comes from. The ideal supplier will know the farmers who rear the animals and will be able to tell you about the produce.

Lamb should hang for 7–10 days, mutton for about 21 days; 19th-century cooks considered that it should hang for as long as possible. Look for firm, dull red lean meat in lamb and dull brownish-red in mutton, with hard white fat and small bones. Avoid excessive fat.

Sheep are cut into fore- and hindquarters. The hindquarter includes the leg (known in Scotland as the gigot, pronounced 'jiggot'), a favourite roasting joint that weighs 2–3.5kg (4½–7¾lb), depending on the breed and age of the animal. It is usually possible to buy a half leg, which means you have to choose between a round piece of lean meat, or a longer, slimmer shank end, with smaller muscles, but sweeter meat. The loin (which together with the leg makes a haunch) is also a good roasting joint, but since it is usually cut into chops, this has to be ordered.

The forequarter includes the 'best end', or rack of lamb. This is a very good small roasting joint, with a neat appearance when nicely trimmed; make sure it is chined (the backbone removed) and that the long bones are divided at the joints to make it easy to separate them. The shoulder contains the bladebone and the long bone adjoining it, plus a knuckle. Bonier and fattier than leg, it is a good roasting joint with a sweeter flavour, and is cheaper. A whole shoulder will generally weigh 2–2.5kg (4½–5½lb), up to 3–3.5kg (6½–7¾lb) for mutton, but it is often sold cut diagonally in half. Finally, the breast – a cut taken from the ends of the ribs – can also be used for roasting. It tends to be chewy, as it contains thin sheets of muscle interspersed with connective tissue, and is also fatty, but has a good flavour and is inexpensive.

As with beef, the question of rare or well done is down to personal preference. For those who are undecided, leg and best end are probably both better cooked on the rare side, but shoulder benefits from being fully cooked – this will cook out some of the fat and crisp up the skin.

For individual recipes, I have given specific temperatures and approximate times, but if all you want is a plain roast joint of lamb or mutton, times and temperatures for fast roasting are similar to those for beef, although I would start it at a slightly lower temperature.

For a fast roast, give the meat 20 minutes at 220°C, 425°F, Gas mark 7, then reduce the heat to 180°C, 350°F, Gas mark 4 and cook for the following times:

- On the bone: 15 minutes per 500g (rare); 18–20 minutes per 500g (medium); 25 minutes per 500g (well done).
- Boneless: 12 minutes per 500g (rare); 13–15 minutes per 500g (medium); 20 minutes per 500g (well done).

For slow roasting, which works well with leg of mutton, cook at 150°C, 300°F, Gas mark 2 for the entire time, allowing 60 minutes per 500g. For breast of lamb or mutton, see recipe on page 56.

Roast Leg of Mutton with Anchovies and Orange Peel

SERVES 8

3kg (6½lb) leg of mutton,
    bone in
1 tablespoon olive oil
2 large garlic cloves, peeled
    and each cut into
    2–3 chunks
1 large shallot, peeled
    and quartered
1 bay leaf (optional)
some fresh marjoram
    sprigs (optional)
½ teaspoon salt
200ml (7fl oz) red wine
200ml (7fl oz) well-flavoured
    stock
2 tablespoons plain flour

FOR THE LARDING

8–10 anchovy fillets preserved
    in oil, drained
1 large orange (preferably
    unwaxed)
18–20 fresh rosemary sprigs,
    about 3cm (1¼in) long

Cut the anchovy fillets into strips about 2cm (¾in) long and 5mm (¼in) wide. Pare the zest from the orange to make about 20–25 strips of zest. Keep the orange – you'll need the juice later.

Take the mutton and use a sharp knife to make parallel rows of small incisions, about 4cm (1½in) apart, from the broad end to the shank. Make a row, with rosemary sprigs in each incision; in the second row, pieces of anchovy; in the third, slivers of orange zest. Repeat until the larding ingredients have been used up.

Preheat the oven to 170°C, 325°F, Gas mark 3. Put the olive oil in a roasting tin. Add the garlic and shallot, the bay leaf and the marjoram. Sit the meat on top and sprinkle with salt. Cook in the preheated oven for about 2 hours, then pour the red wine and the juice of the orange into the roasting tin and return to roast for a further 1½ hours, until the juices run clear. Put the joint on a warm plate, cover loosely with foil, and leave to rest.

Pour all the roasting juices out of the tin into a bowl and allow the fat to rise; skim off as much as possible and reserve. Put the roasting tin over a low heat. Stir in half the stock, scraping the tin to incorporate all the residue, and add to the reserved juices. Return the tin to the heat and add 2–3 tablespoons of the meat fat. Stir in the flour and allow to brown lightly, but not burn. Strain the cooking juices into the tin, stirring, and bring to the boil to make a lightly thickened gravy. Add the remainder of the stock, taste, and check the seasoning.

Shoulder of Mutton with or without Oysters

This recipe uses shoulder of lamb, or preferably mutton. I have suggested a boned one, seasoned inside, but a bone-in shoulder can be used if you wish, seasoned on the surface. The oysters will add a mild but not obviously fishy note. Without them, this is still a good recipe, based on one suggested by Robert May in his book The Accomplish't Cook *(1660), a wonderful compendium of recipes.*

SERVES 6

1 shoulder of mutton, 2–2.5kg
(4½–5½lb), boned weight
1 tablespoon finely chopped
fresh marjoram
zest of 1 lemon (preferably
unwaxed), grated
a pinch of freshly grated
nutmeg
½ teaspoon salt
250ml (9fl oz) dry white wine
12 oysters (optional)
1 small shallot, peeled and
finely chopped
1 tablespoon plain flour
stock or water, to taste

If the butcher has rolled and tied the meat, cut the string and unroll. Scatter over the marjoram, lemon zest, a generous grating of nutmeg and the salt. Re-roll and tie firmly.

Preheat the oven to 220°C, 425°F, Gas mark 7. To calculate the cooking time, see page 49. Put the meat into a roasting tin and cook for about 30 minutes. Baste with the wine, sprinkle the surface of the meat with salt, and reduce the heat to 180°C, 350°F, Gas mark 4. Continue to cook until done to your taste. Baste with the cooking juices at intervals.

When the meat is done, remove to a warmed serving plate and leave to rest. Pour all the roasting juices out of the tin into a bowl and allow the fat to rise; skim off as much as possible and reserve.

If using, open the oysters, strain their liquor through a sieve lined with kitchen paper to catch any bits of shell or sand, and reserve in a separate bowl. Add about 2 tablespoons of the fat back to the roasting tin, heat gently and cook the chopped shallot in it until translucent. Add the flour and continue stirring and cooking until lightly browned. Stir in the roasting juices to make a smooth gravy. If using oysters, add their liquor at this point, stirring, and bring to a simmer. Just before serving, stir in the oysters and continue to cook until thoroughly hot. Otherwise, proceed as for a conventional gravy, adding a little stock and season to taste.

Rack of Lamb with a Herb Crust

The rack, or best end of neck of lamb, consists of 6–8 cutlets joined together, with the backbone removed. Often the ends of the bones are cleaned of all meat, and sometimes decorated with paper frills. Two racks presented with the bones making a crisscross formation are known as a guard of honour; three, curved and stitched together vertically so that the meat is inside and the bones radiate in a sunburst, is a crown roast, which was very fashionable during the 1970s.

A lone rack of lamb is a good joint for 2–3 people (although don't expect leftovers), and also one that is nice cold; the coating of breadcrumbs recalls 17th- and 18th-century 'dredges' of flavoured crumbs.

SERVES 2–3

1 rack of lamb, trimmed
1 fresh rosemary sprig
30g (1oz) fresh white
    breadcrumbs
2 tablespoons chopped parsley
1 tablespoon chopped basil
1 garlic clove, peeled
    and crushed
½ teaspoon salt

Preheat the oven to 180°C, 350°F, Gas mark 4.

Remove the parchment-like skin covering the meat (a thin layer of fat should remain) and scrape the bones clean if the butcher hasn't done this for you. Put the lamb, bones down, in a small roasting tin or ovenproof dish, tucking the rosemary underneath. Roast for 30–40 minutes, depending on the size of the rack.

While the lamb cooks, mix the breadcrumbs, parsley, basil, garlic and salt. After the initial roasting, remove the meat from the oven and turn up the heat to 200°C, 400°F, Gas mark 6. Carefully spread the breadcrumb and herb mixture over the fat layer, pressing it down well. Roast for another 10 minutes.

This roast does not produce any gravy worth speaking of, so if you wish to serve it hot, good accompaniments are those which add moisture, such as Boulangère Potatoes (see page 199) or a dish of baked tomatoes.

Slow-Roast Mutton and Salsa Verde

This recipe was originally created for Herdwick mutton; these sheep, born with black pelts that turn grey or rusty brown as they grow, have distinctive pale heads, small curved horns, and are principally found on the highest of the Lake District fells. Beatrix Potter had her own Herdwick flock at Hill Top Farm; it is still a working farm and the National Trust tenant keeps a flock of Herdwicks. Meat from other breeds will work equally well. Salsa verde, which includes both capers and mint, recalls the English traditions of caper sauce with mutton and mint sauce with lamb.

SERVES 6–8

a whole leg of mutton, bone in
salt

FOR THE SALSA VERDE
a good handful each of fresh
    mint, parsley and basil
1 small garlic clove, peeled
    and crushed
2 tablespoons capers, rinsed
    of any salt or vinegar in
    which they have been
    preserved
2 tablespoons Dijon mustard
2 tablespoons red wine
    vinegar
8 tablespoons olive oil

Salt the meat lightly and cook in a very low oven, 140°C, 275°F, Gas mark 1, allowing 60 minutes per 500g.

To make the salsa verde, wash the herbs and pick off the leaves, discarding the stalks. Blend all the ingredients together, taste and season.

Carve the mutton and serve the sauce separately.

Breast of Lamb Stuffed with Capers, Garlic and Herbs

Breast of lamb is something the Victorians would have described as being suitable for family meals. It needs slow cooking, moisture, and a highly flavoured stuffing to add interest and counteract the fattiness. In the past, standard English mixtures of bread with herbs and suet bound with eggs were favoured, but these are very dense to modern tastes. I suggest using a mixture with flavours borrowed from salsa verde (capers, herbs), which works well with this meat.

SERVES 3–4

2 breasts of lamb, boned

40g (1½oz) unsalted butter

1 medium onion, peeled and finely chopped

2 garlic cloves, peeled and crushed

2 tablespoons salted capers, well rinsed and coarsely chopped

a little chopped fresh mint

3 tablespoons finely chopped fresh parsley

1 large tablespoon chopped fresh basil

zest of ½ lemon (preferably unwaxed), finely grated

150g (5oz) crustless day-old white bread, torn into small pieces

splash of stock or milk, to moisten

Breast of lamb is flattish and thin, with one straight edge cut from the forequarter, which may still contain the ends of the rib bones, unless the butcher has already removed them. If you have to do this yourself, run a knife in between the bones and the meat on the outside, then cut them away from the lesser covering inside and slip them out.

To make the stuffing, melt the butter over a low heat and fry the onion and garlic until softened. Stir in the capers, herbs, lemon zest and bread, and add enough stock or milk to moisten the bread.

Spread the meat out, skin-side down. Put a layer of stuffing on top of each piece, then roll from the narrow end and firmly tie at each end with string.

Preheat the oven to 140°C, 275°F, Gas mark 1. Put the lamb in a shallow roasting tin and cook for 3–3½ hours, pouring off any fat that the meat renders. Then turn the oven up to 200°C, 400°F, Gas mark 6, and give it a further 15 minutes to crisp up.

It will not produce gravy, but a light tomato sauce goes well with the caper-flavoured stuffing. Alternatively, serve a salad dressed with vinaigrette on the side.

Dried Apricot and Almond Stuffing

While lamb or mutton cooked on the bone scores best for flavour, it is not the easiest thing to carve. Both leg and shoulder are often boned, creating joints ideal for stuffing. Stuff the joint, then roll and tie with string. Or, if using a boned shoulder, tie it as a 'cushion' – in four, like a parcel – or as a 'melon' – manoeuvre the stuffed meat into a rough ball shape, then take a long piece of string and wrap it four times round the meat, crossing at the poles, giving the appearance of eight sections like a cantaloupe melon. Carve a rolled joint into slices, and a cushion or melon into sections.

SERVES 3–4

40g (1½oz) unsalted butter

1 small onion, peeled and very finely chopped

50g (2oz) almonds, blanched and cut into slivers

150g (5oz) crustless day-old white bread, torn into small pieces

75g (3oz) dried apricots, soaked for a few hours, then drained and roughly chopped

zest of ½ lemon (preferably unwaxed), finely grated

a generous pinch of freshly grated nutmeg

½ teaspoon salt

freshly ground black pepper

50–100ml (2–3½fl oz) stock or milk

Melt the butter in a small frying pan and sauté the onion gently until translucent. Toast the almonds lightly in the oven for 5–10 minutes; watch to make sure they don't burn. In a bowl, combine the onion, almonds, bread, apricots and lemon zest. Season with a generous grating of nutmeg, the salt and some pepper. Mix well and pour in just enough stock or milk to make the bread moist but not soggy.

Use to stuff the cavity left by boning the joint and roast. To calculate the cooking time and temperature, see page 49. Alternatively, make into small balls and bake in a lightly greased dish for about 20–30 minutes at 180°C, 350°F, Gas mark 4.

Cucumber Chutney

Cold lamb and mutton need strongly flavoured accompaniments. Pickles and chutneys, especially fruity ones such as apple or apricot, are good options. Another is a fresh chutney of the type routinely made in Indian cookery. While not 'traditional' to English food, these were appreciated by colonial administrators living in India during the British Raj. The original recipe was given in a book called Common-Sense Cookery (1905). Its author, Colonel Kenney-Herbert, was an army officer in India who wrote several cookery books in the late 19th century. His book expresses a sense of military precision combined with exasperation at the ways of Indian cooks and a desire to keep a good, if possibly somewhat extravagant, table. The only green herbs he used were parsley and chives, where we, and probably the Indian original, would add green coriander – a flavour not popular among the Victorian English. Make this just before you want to eat it.

SERVES 3–4

5cm (2in) length of cucumber
a pinch of granulated sugar
1 dessertspoon white
    wine vinegar
about 1 tablespoon finely
    chopped herbs – a
    combination of two or
    more of the following:
    chives, parsley, coriander,
    mint
a small piece of fresh hot
    green chilli pepper (or to
    taste), finely chopped
1 dessertspoon olive oil
salt and pepper

Peel the cucumber and cut in half crossways, then cut both pieces into slim julienne strips. Dissolve the sugar in the vinegar and pour over the cucumber. Stir in the chopped herbs, chilli pepper and olive oil. Season to taste.

Serve with slices of cold roast lamb or mutton and a salad of bitter leaves, lightly dressed with lemon juice and olive oil.

Laver Sauce

Laver, or laverbread (Porphyra umbilicalis), is often known by its Japanese name, nori. This seaweed, washed and cooked for a very long time to make a soft, greenish-black purée, is a traditional food of the south Wales coast. In the past, it was also collected from the Somerset and Devon coast. A good fishmonger may be able to get some for you, or you can look online. It makes a good sauce for a plainly roasted leg or shoulder of mutton or lamb, especially saltmarsh lamb.

SERVES 4

75g (3oz) unsalted butter
450g (1lb) prepared laverbread
juice of 1 Seville orange
salt and pepper

Melt the butter in a saucepan, add the laverbread and stir gently until hot. Squeeze in the orange juice. Taste and adjust the seasoning with a little salt and pepper if you consider it necessary.

If Seville oranges are unobtainable, use a mixture of lemon juice and sweet orange juice instead.

Mint Sauce

By the mid-20th century, mint sauce was the preferred accompaniment for lamb, combining two elements that go well with this meat – a strongly aromatic perfume and a sharp taste. For mint sauce lovers, Eliza Acton's recipe of 3 heaped teaspoons of finely chopped young fresh mint, 2 heaped teaspoons of caster sugar and 6 teaspoons of 'the best vinegar' (try a good white wine one) is a good formula. Stir together until the sugar has dissolved.

LEFTOVERS

The key to making the most of leftover lamb or mutton is to make sure any skin, gristle and fat is removed. It's perfect for a classic Shepherd's Pie (see opposite).

SCOTCH BROTH

Stock from lamb or mutton bones has a distinctive flavour, best used with robust vegetable combinations found in the Scotch Broth tradition.

SERVES 4

1 litre (1¾ pints) stock made with the bones
    from a lamb or mutton roast
40g (1½oz) split peas (yellow or green),
    soaked overnight
40g (1½oz) pearl barley
2 medium carrots, scraped and sliced
1 small turnip, about 75g (3oz), peeled
    and chopped
1 leek, trimmed and chopped
1 celery stick, chopped
a few leaves of curly kale, shredded
salt and pepper
about 1 tablespoon chopped parsley

Put the stock in a pan and add the soaked split peas, barley and all the vegetables except the kale. Simmer gently until the peas and barley are soft. Add the kale and cook for about 10 minutes longer. Check the seasoning and add salt and pepper as needed.

Divide the broth between bowls and add parsley just before serving.

SHEPHERD'S (OR COTTAGE) PIE

This dish, a standard method for using up leftover roast lamb or mutton, first appeared in the 1870s, when mincing machines were developed. Cottage pie is the name usually given to a beef version. This is a basic recipe for either beef or lamb.

SERVES 4

1 tablespoon fat from the roast, or oil
1 large onion, peeled and finely chopped
1 garlic clove, peeled and crushed
450–500g (1–1lb 2oz) cold roast meat (remove any skin, gristle, most of the fat and any bits of herbs left over from roasting)
300ml (10fl oz) leftover gravy, plus a little stock
salt and pepper
about 1 tablespoon chopped parsley

FOR THE TOPPING
1kg (2¼lb) floury potatoes
200ml (7fl oz) milk
30–40g (1–1½oz) unsalted butter
salt and pepper

Heat the fat in a large frying pan and add the onion and garlic. Let it cook gently without browning for 10–15 minutes. Chop the meat finely, or put it through a mincing machine (this produces a softer texture). Add the meat to the pan with the onion. Stir well and add the gravy, plus a little stock (or water) if the mixture seems dry. Taste for seasoning, adding salt and pepper as necessary, then add some chopped parsley. Lightly grease an ovenproof dish and pour in the meat mixture.

For the topping, peel the potatoes, chop roughly and boil until just tender. Drain and mash with the milk, butter, salt and pepper.

Preheat the oven to 190°C, 375°F, Gas mark 5. Cover the meat with the mashed potato, roughening the surface with a fork. Brown in the oven for about 30 minutes, or leave to go cold and reheat (same temperature).

If you are cooking the beef version, Cottage Pie, try stirring 2–3 teaspoons of truffle oil into the mashed potato and sprinkle the top with grated cheese, such as strong Cheddar or Parmesan. Cook as above.

PILAF

I first encountered the idea of a pilaf in Elizabeth David's Mediterranean Food *(1950), although lamb and rice dishes appear in English cookery books as early as the 17th century. It's a good method for stretching a small amount of leftover meat, or using up an odd slice or two in a dish for one person. Ingredients and quantities depend to some extent on the contents of the refrigerator and your appetite: the following are suggestions.*

SERVES 4

75–100g (3–4oz) long-grain rice
1 tablespoon pine nuts or blanched almonds,
    cut into slivers
1 tablespoon olive oil
¼–½ medium onion, peeled and chopped
1 garlic clove, peeled and sliced
75g (3oz) cooked mutton or lamb, cut into
    small chunks, with any skin, gristle and
    large pieces of fat removed
about 1 tablespoon raisins and currants, mixed
1 large ripe tomato, skinned and sliced,
    or 1–2 tablespoons passata
salt and pepper

Boil the rice according to your favourite method.

Toast the nuts lightly in a heated frying pan, then set aside. Add the oil to the pan and fry the onion gently. Add the garlic, and continue to cook until the onion is translucent. Add the meat, and continue to fry gently. Add the raisins and currants, and keep stirring; after a moment, add the nuts. Finally, stir in the tomato or passata.

By now, the rice should be cooked. Drain if necessary and stir in the meat mixture. Leave covered for a few minutes, then serve with natural yoghurt or Cucumber Chutney (see page 60). Some Crisp Fried Browned Onions (see page 210) make a good garnish, or add 1 tablespoon chopped parsley.

PILAF STUFFING
To make a stuffing, use 200g (7oz) rice, and omit the meat and tomato. Use butter in place of the oil, and add pine nuts, currants and chopped parsley to flavour, or almonds and apricots (see page 59).

Pork, Ham
& Gammon

Pork comes from porkers. This may seem a statement of the obvious, but pigs are graded by age and weight. A porker is a relatively young pig, which has achieved the optimum weight for fresh meat but is not large enough for salting for bacon and ham (for that, one needs, naturally, a baconer). Pigs for fresh pork can be grown on to be older and heavier, but as with all animal rearing, the economics of feed versus the return on the meat come into play. In some cultures, pork is taboo, but to the poor of the British Isles, and much of Europe, it often provided the small amount of meat they ate for most of the year. Pigs breed fast and have large litters, and a piglet could be acquired for relatively little money. In towns, they were fed on household scraps and what they could scavenge in the street (in spite of the authorities' attempts to control them, pigs were a common sight in the streets of many towns until the early 18th century).

In the countryside they might have been confined in a sty, or allowed a freer range: pannage, the autumn feeding of pigs on acorns and beechmast in woodland, declined after the Middle Ages, although if you visit the New Forest between September and November you may still see pigs roaming free. Pigs had their place, too, in the wider rural economy, especially in cheese-making areas, where they consumed the whey left over from this process. In short, these were useful animals, quick providers of meat in restricted space, for relatively little outlay.

This does not mean that the rural poor ate roast pork every Sunday. For a start, fresh pork was considered dangerous in summer, well into the 19th century. The meat does not keep well in hot weather, and effective refrigeration did not develop until the 1880s. Pigs were killed only during the cooler months of the year – the rule of thumb being only when there is an 'r' in the month (like oysters). In addition, most of the meat was salted for hams and bacon. These were stored and used slowly throughout the year, until the next pig was ready for the kill, although the hams were often sold to pay various household expenses, including the acquisition of the next piglet.

The fresh pork that the poor got under this system was usually the offcuts from baconers. The better-off, who could afford to buy meat, might acquire the cuts we are familiar with, but recipes for roasting pork in British culinary traditions are few and mostly simple. Favourite cuts seem to have been leg of pork and griskin – the lean part of the loin.

In the mid-19th century, Eliza Acton observed of roast pork that it 'is not at the present day much served at very good tables, particularly in this form', which may have reflected a general and longstanding feeling that it was not the most elegant of meats. She also commented on the 'old savoury stuffing of sage and onions', showing that this combination – still the one that springs most readily to mind when roast pork and English culinary traditions are mentioned – was considered a tradition even then.

Suckling pig was a different matter – special food. It was uneconomic to kill such a young and potentially productive animal for food (they were considered best at 3–4 weeks old). However, in communities whose ability to store fresh meat was limited, but which had ready access to live animals, a suckling pig represented a luxury meal on the hoof. Given that a sow can have two or three litters a year, and breeds all year round, there was always likely to be one such pig available – and it could be cooked as soon as it was dressed (in 1756, Martha Bradley said it was best killed on the morning of the day it was to be cooked). Properly roasted, it provided an exquisite combination of tender, mildly flavoured meat with delicately crisp skin – and as with all relatively large and spectacular pieces of meat, it had extra status.

Roasting a suckling pig in front of an open fire required a great deal of attention to make sure the entire animal cooked evenly. They are long, and made even longer by the habit of trussing them with their front legs forward and hind legs back, thus requiring a fireplace that was also long. There was also the possibility that the plumper mid-section, closer to the fire than the slender little trotters, would be cooked through and scorching while the extremities were still raw. To counteract this, a special shield known as a pig-iron was sometimes suspended from the fire grate to lessen the heat received by the pig's midriff.

Of the meat that was salted, most bacon was used in the form of rashers to flavour other foods, and was enjoyed by both rich and poor. Hams, though, were a high-status item, which might be cooked whole to make an appearance on the tables of the wealthy. Usually they were boiled, but roasting and baking were sometimes preferred. Both gammon and ham refer to the hind leg of a pig above the hock joint, cured by salting and drying, but there seems to have been a distinction in the past: a ham was cured as a separate piece of meat, whereas a gammon seems to have been left attached to a bacon flitch and cured as part of the side – a trickier process because of the varying thicknesses of meat involved. The words now seem to be used more or less interchangeably, although gammon sometimes implies a milder cure. Traditionally meat was cured with only salt, but today potassium nitrate and sodium nitrate are also used. These give the ham and bacon their pink colour, but have been linked to increased risk of cancer.

Buying Pork

Pork, like beef and lamb, has been bred for lean meat over the past 40 years or so. Pork that is very lean is dull in flavour and dry in texture, but no one wants to pay for large amounts of fat. To produce really good pork, as with other meat, a balance has to be struck. Tradition – a breed that might have roamed the apple orchards of the south-west – conflicts with the economics of bringing an animal to the optimum weight for meat in the shortest possible time with the highest proportion of lean prime meat. Some butchers make a point of sourcing meat from slower-growing traditional and rare breeds, because the slower growth means more flavour. What the pig eats also makes a difference, both to flavour and to the texture of the fat.

Another factor in the flavour of pork is something called 'boar taint'. While male cattle and some sheep destined for meat are castrated, in Britain, male pigs are left intact, and this can lead to a distinctive flavour in the meat. Musky is a polite way to describe it. The issues behind this relate both to animal welfare and commercial implications to do with the way the animal gains weight. The theory is that taint will not be a problem since pigs are slaughtered for pork before puberty (when boar taint develops, as a result of hormonal changes). However, other factors operate: some pigs have more of the flavour, or enter puberty at a younger than average age, while some people are more sensitive to the flavour. The only way to counter this problem is to know your supplier, and to avoid the problem entirely you will either have to buy meat from female pigs, or find a supplier who castrates the males (important for traditional breeds that are grown on to be older than average).

When buying pork, look for lean meat that is pale pink, moist but firm; the fat should be white, firm but tender and present in reasonable but not excessive amounts. To store, remove shop wrappings, cover loosely and place on a plate or tray in the coolest part of the refrigerator.

Flavourings

Stuffing, including that old-fashioned mixture of sage and onion (see page 198) is sometimes used for flavour and to counteract dryness in cuts such as leg. Other flavourings for pork tend to fall into three categories: fruity, aromatic and sweet. In Britain, apple sauce or baked apples are especially good with a well-produced traditional-breed meat, the sweetness of the apple picking up on the inherent sweet note of well-fed pork. Lemon zest is also a good flavouring for pork, especially with rosemary, thyme, fennel, garlic and black pepper. Chinese culture has provided a different range of flavourings, such as star anise, five-spice powder and soy sauce in combinations with sugar or honey. These go particularly well with slow-roast pork. Traditionally the British have not marinated pork, but if you are using aromatic herbs, sprinkle them over the meat and rub in some time before roasting (even the night before).

Cuts for Roasting and Roasting Times

Because the lean is tender and the fat usually ample, most cuts of pork are suitable for roasting. The loin and leg contain the highest proportion of lean meat in large muscles. A whole leg of pork is a big joint that tends to be dry if not carefully cooked. Forequarter cuts tend to be fattier and have more connective tissue, but they still roast well, especially slowly. If it's crackling that you want, choose a piece of loin, a joint fairly even in shape along its entire length; it can produce spectacular results. Loin, as with other animals, has a long tender undercut (often sold separately as fillet); if you are fortunate, it will be left in place, an extra treat.

Most people would consider removing the skin to be a waste, but you will need to do this if you want a less fatty result, or to marinate the meat. The skin on all pork joints should be scored, to help it crisp and make it easy to divide after cooking – most butchers will do this for you.

Pork should always be thoroughly cooked. A rule of thumb for all cuts is to start the meat at 230°C, 450°F, Gas mark 8 for 20 minutes, then reduce the heat to 170°C, 325°F, Gas mark 3 and allow 25 minutes per 500g for prime cuts (leg, loin) or 30 minutes per 500g for other cuts. I prefer to cook belly pork and forequarter cuts on slow, 140°C, 275°F, Gas mark 1 for 60 minutes per 500g.

A meat thermometer is useful when cooking ham or gammon. Because these are cured meats, they remain pink even when fully cooked, and it is less easy to tell when they are done.

Crackling

How to get crackling to crackle is, to some extent, a matter of knowing your oven and working out the optimum time and temperature. Slow roasting is a more reliable way of producing crackling than fast roasting, simply because it gives the skin longer to crisp up and is less likely to scorch the edges of the joint. A method frequently recommended – at least since the 19th century – is to rub the skin of pork with olive oil and salt before cooking.

Whatever method is used, three points help to provide good results. The first is that the meat must have a reasonable covering of fat: look for a layer just over 1cm (½in) thick, certainly not less. The next is that the skin should be properly scored; this needs to be done neatly in parallel lines at intervals of about 1cm (½in) apart, to about the same depth. The cuts might go down to the lean, but should not penetrate it. A good butcher will do this if you ask. The third point is that the skin should be dry when the meat is put into the oven. This makes the following method, derived from Chinese cookery, seem rather strange, but it does work:

Put the pork, skin-side up, on a rack in the sink. Boil a kettleful of water and immediately pour the water evenly over the skin, allowing it to drain straight away. The skin will mostly dry quickly as the residual hot water evaporates, but blot it with kitchen paper or a clean cloth to make absolutely sure. Then salt and roast as normal.

If the meat is cooked and the diners assembling, but the crackling has failed to crisp up, free it – as a sheet – from the meat and leave the latter to rest. Put the crackling in a roasting tin and return it to a moderately hot oven, 200°C, 400°F, Gas mark 6, for 5–10 minutes. Cut it into strips using scissors.

Roast Loin of Pork
with Sage and Onion Puddings

SERVES 6

a piece of pork loin, about
    2.5kg (5½lb)
150ml (5fl oz) dry white wine
generous 1 tablespoon
    plain flour
250ml (9fl oz) stock (pork
    or chicken)
salt and pepper

FOR THE PUDDINGS
pork or beef dripping
    for frying, and for the
    pudding tins
1 small onion, peeled and
    chopped
half the quantities given for
    Yorkshire Pudding (see
    page 29)
12 sage leaves, chopped

Preheat the oven to 230°C, 450°F, Gas mark 8. Prepare the pork for roasting in a tin. Calculate the roasting time. Roast for 20 minutes, then reduce the heat to 170°C, 325°F, Gas mark 3. After about 1 hour, add the white wine to the tin.

Meanwhile, prepare the sage and onion puddings. Melt the fat in a frying pan and cook the onion gently until translucent. Turn off the heat and allow to cool.

Cook the meat until done, checking from time to time. Remove from the oven and allowed to rest for at least 20 minutes before carving. Turn up the heat to 220°C, 425°F, Gas mark 7.

Make the Yorkshire pudding batter, then stir in the cooled onion and the chopped sage. Using a muffin tray or deep-holed bun tin, put 1 scant teaspoon of fat in each mould and then put into the oven to heat. When the fat is smoking hot, take the muffin tray out and add 1–2cm (½–¾in) to each mould. Return to the oven and cook for 15–20 minutes, or until puffed and golden, and done in the middle.

To make the gravy, pour all the juices out of the roasting tin into a bowl. Set aside for a few minutes then remove as much fat as possible to a separate container.

Put about 2 tablespoons of the fat back into the roasting tin and add the flour. Stir well over low heat, allowing the flour to brown. Stir in the juices, scraping up any residue stuck to the tin. Gradually add the stock (you may not need it all), stirring well, and bring to the boil. Season to taste.

Pork with Garlic and Herb Paste

The idea of cutting off the skin and putting a deeply flavoured paste under it before cooking came via a friend (thanks, Caroline). The seasonings are mostly ones associated with traditional pork sausages in Britain, with garlic, mint and lemon to give the mixture a lift. For an inexpensive roast, use belly pork, provided it is fairly thick and has a good layer of fat between the skin and lean. The original recipe used pork loin, and if you want to try this, follow the times and temperatures on page 70.

SERVES 4

a piece of belly pork,
    weighing about 2kg (4½lb)
1 tablespoon each of finely
    chopped fresh sage,
    rosemary and mint,
    finely chopped
8 garlic cloves, peeled
    and crushed
grated zest of 1 lemon
    (preferably unwaxed)
a good pinch of finely
    ground allspice
a good pinch of finely
    ground coriander
1–2 tablespoons olive oil
1 teaspoon salt
a generous grind of
    black pepper
a splash of white wine
    or stock
1 tablespoon plain flour

Put the pork on a board and carefully cut through the fat layer between the skin and the meat (it helps if the pork is well chilled). Aim to leave just under 1cm (½in) fat attached. Keep the skin on one side and put the meat, bones down, in a roasting tin.

Mix all the ingredients except the white wine and flour to make a paste. Spread this evenly over the top of the meat. Put the skin back on top. Leave to marinate for 2–3 hours.

Preheat the oven to 140°C, 275°F, Gas mark 1 and put the pork in to cook. Allow at least 60 minutes per 500g, possibly a little longer. It will yield a lot of fat and some deep-brown juices.

When the meat is cooked, remove it to a warmed plate. If the crackling hasn't crisped, put it in a shallow tin, turn the oven up to 200°C, 400°F, Gas mark 6 and return it to cook for 10–15 minutes, checking progress occasionally. Pour off all the fat and juices from the roasting tin into a bowl. Deglaze the tin with white wine or stock and add to the juices. Skim off the fat.

Put 2 tablespoons of fat back into the roasting tin and add a little flour, stirring with a wooden spoon over a low heat. Allow the flour to cook and brown a little, then stir in the cooking juices, and a little more stock if necessary, to produce gravy.

To serve, slice the meat and serve with cabbage and potatoes.

Slow-Roast Belly Pork with Root Vegetables and Oriental Flavours

SERVES 4

about 1.5kg (3½lb) belly pork, skin scored

2–3 large baking potatoes

1 large carrot

1 sweet potato

2 large parsnips

2–3 small white turnips, or about one-third of a larger yellow turnip

about 1 tablespoon oil

fresh root ginger, about 2cm (¾in), peeled and cut into long matchsticks

a few shallots, peeled and halved lengthways

6–8 garlic cloves, peeled

salt

FOR THE ORIENTAL FLAVOURS

2–3 whole star anise

1 teaspoon whole black peppercorns, crushed

40g (1½oz) honey

2 tablespoons soy sauce

2 tablespoons dry sherry

200–300ml (7–10fl oz) chicken stock (keep about a third of this back for the end)

Preheat the oven to 220°C, 425°F, Gas mark 7. Give the pork the boiling water treatment (see page 71), and salt lightly. Mix all the oriental flavourings in a small bowl. Wash, trim and peel all root vegetables. Cut into chunks. Put them in a pan, cover with cold water and bring to the boil for about 2 minutes. Drain thoroughly. Heat the oil in a roasting tin until very hot, add the vegetables and turn them. Mix in the ginger, shallots and garlic. Pour over the flavourings and put the pork on top, skin-side up.

Roast for 15 minutes, then reduce the heat to 150°C, 300°F, Gas mark 2. Cook for 2–3 hours; stir the vegetables once or twice.

About 30 minutes before you want to eat, turn the heat back up to 200°C, 400°F, Gas mark 6. Stir the vegetables, then return the tin to the oven. When the crackling is crisp, remove the meat to a warmed serving platter. Arrange the vegetables around it. Keep hot.

Skim the fat off the juices left in the roasting tin. Taste and add more salt if needed. Use hot stock to thin and deglaze any residue in the tin, then pour all juices into a gravy boat.

PORK, HAM & GAMMON

75

Loin of Pork Stuffed with Spinach

SERVES 4

1kg (2¼lb) boned pork loin
a little lemon zest (preferably unwaxed), finely grated
salt and pepper
1 tablespoon olive oil

FOR THE SPINACH STUFFING
250g (9oz) spinach, thick stems removed
50g (2oz) parsley, stems removed
½ teaspoon salt
freshly ground black pepper

Buy a piece of pork loin with a good proportion of lean meat. Remove the skin with the fat beneath, plus the 'tail' of fatty meat. The lean meat has a thin white covering of sinew over one side. Use a sharp knife to separate it from the lean neatly.

Place the meat so that the grain is at right angles to you. Take a sharp knife and make a cut into the left side, parallel to the grain and about one-third of the way down from the top. Don't cut all the way through – leave a 'hinge' at the right-hand side. Now start at the right-hand side and repeat the action, cutting about one-third of the way up from the bottom, leaving the 'hinge' at the left.

Open out the meat as a single sheet. Sandwich it between two pieces of greaseproof paper and beat with a rolling pin until it is roughly 1½–2 times larger, and about half the original thickness. Season with the lemon zest and salt and coarsely ground black pepper. Put aside while you make the stuffing.

Wash the spinach and pack into a saucepan. Cook over high heat for a couple of minutes, stirring until it has wilted. Add the parsley and cook just enough to soften it. Remove from the heat, press into a sieve to get rid of the liquid. Put the mixture onto a board and chop coarsely. Season with the salt and pepper.

Spread the spinach and parsley mixture over the meat, leaving about 2.5cm (1in) all round. Roll up and tie firmly with string. Preheat the oven to 200°C, 400°F, Gas mark 6. Put the olive oil in a small roasting tin, then add the meat and roast for about 50 minutes. Make sure the outside isn't cooking too fast, and season with salt halfway through cooking. Carve into thin slices.

Pork Marinated to Taste like Wild Boar

SERVES 6–8

2.5–3kg (5½–6½lb) leg of pork,
  boned and skinned
400ml (14fl oz) pork, chicken
  or veal stock
3 tablespoons plain flour
salt and pepper

FOR THE MARINADE

300ml (10fl oz) red wine
50ml (2fl oz) red wine vinegar
½ onion, peeled and sliced
2 shallots, peeled and sliced
2 garlic cloves, peeled
  and crushed
3 bay leaves, crushed
8–10 thyme sprigs
a few parsley stalks,
  roughly chopped
12 black peppercorns, bruised
12 juniper berries, bruised
3 cloves, bruised
zest of ½ orange (preferably
  unwaxed), cut in long
  strips
1 teaspoon salt

Put all the marinade ingredients in a saucepan and bring to the boil. Allow to cool.

Lightly score the fat of the meat in a diamond pattern. Put it in a deep bowl, and pour the cooled marinade over the meat. Turn it in the mixture, then cover and store in the refrigerator, where it can marinate for up to 4 days. Turn the meat a couple of times each day.

When ready to cook, preheat the oven to 220°C, 425°F, Gas mark 7. Remove the meat from the marinade. Strain the latter, reserving the liquid. Put the meat on a rack in a roasting tin and add a little water to the base of the tin. Cook for 20 minutes, then reduce the heat to 170°C, 325°F, Gas mark 3 for a further 2 hours, or until done. Baste with the reserved marinade at intervals and check that the liquid in the tin doesn't burn. If it becomes too deep brown, add a little more water to the tin – the gravy is very rich but will burn easily.

When the meat is cooked, remove to a warm serving dish and allow it to rest. Pour all the fat and juices from the tin into a bowl, then deglaze the tin with a little of the stock and add this to the juices. The fat will rise to the surface – skim off as much as possible. Put about 3 tablespoons of the fat back into the tin and sprinkle in the flour. Stir well and allow to cook gently over low heat. Once it has turned a creamy colour, gradually stir in the reserved cooking juices, then the stock. Taste and check the seasoning before serving.

Roast Ham or Gammon

When cooking ham, boiling is often thought of as the standard method, but both spit-roasting and baking were also used. There are two basic ways to finish a ham, either by glazing or by dredging with breadcrumbs, recalling 17th- and 18th-century spit-roasts.

SERVES 8

a piece of uncooked ham or
    gammon, without skin,
    weighing 2kg (4½lb)
a handful of cloves (optional)
a glaze or breadcrumb coating
    (see below and page 82)

Follow the supplier's instructions about whether or not to soak the ham. If the piece of meat is to be served glazed, score the fat in diamonds at about 2cm (¾in) intervals and stud with cloves.

Preheat the oven to 170°C, 325°F, Gas mark 3, then put the meat in a roasting tin and cover with foil. Bake for 30 minutes per 500g, and 30 minutes extra. For the last 30 minutes, remove the foil to allow the outside of the joint to brown, or use one of the finishes over the page.

Glaze for Ham

Where the idea of glazing the exterior of a ham with a shiny, sticky, sweetish finish came from is not clear. Possibly the glaze derives from the use of sweet wines for cooking ham, which seems to have been quite common in the 18th century. This glaze is based on a recipe from the American compendium, The Joy of Cooking, *first published in 1931. The original called for bourbon, which works very well; a blended Scotch is fine.*

125ml (4fl oz) whisky,
    preferably without
    smoky character
125g (4½oz) demerara sugar
zest of ½ orange (unwaxed),
    cut in thin strips
1 piece of star anise (optional)

Mix together all the ingredients, without dissolving the sugar. About 30 minutes before the end of cooking time, remove any covering from the meat and pour this mixture over it. If some of the sugar crystals remain on top, so much the better, because they will crisp a little during cooking. Use the mixture that runs into the tin and combines with the cooking juices to baste the meat at frequent intervals during the remaining cooking time.

Breadcrumb Coating for Ham

John Nott, in The Cook's and Confectioner's Dictionary *(1723), directs that a roasted gammon should be dredged with a mixture of breadcrumbs and finely chopped parsley. This produces a much subtler effect than the slightly alarming crust of cornflake-yellow crumbs now used on industrially produced ham.*

4 tablespoons breadcrumbs
　　made from stale
　　white bread
1 tablespoon very finely
　　chopped parsley

The breadcrumbs are best made by putting a couple of slices of stale white bread in a low oven. Leave them until they are dried out and pale gold, then remove, cool and crush. The crumbs need to be quite fine: pulverise the bread in a food processor or beat it in a mortar to reduce it as much as possible. Then rub through a wire sieve. Most will pass through to become near-powder. A few will remain in the sieve, but the process should reduce these to a degree of fineness that is acceptable, so use these too and mix in the parsley.

Put the mixture on a sheet of greaseproof paper. About 30 minutes before the end of cooking time, remove the foil from the meat and roll the side with the fat on over the crumb mixture, using the paper to help pat it over the surface. Return to the oven and cook for a further 30 minutes or until the coating is golden brown.

Roast Ham with Rhenish Wine

'Rhenish' wine (from the Rhineland vineyards) was much appreciated in Britain during the 17th and 18th centuries. Whether it had the same perfumed notes and degree of sweetness that it does today is not clear, but this recipe, after one given by John Thacker in 1758, is worth trying.

SERVES 6–8

a piece of unsmoked ham
    weighing about 2–2.5kg
    (4½–5½lb)
a handful of cloves (optional)
1 bottle light, medium-sweet
    German wine, such as
    Niersteiner
scant 2 tablespoons plain
    flour
200ml (7fl oz) light stock
salt and pepper

Follow the supplier's instructions about whether or not to soak the ham.

When ready to cook, carefully remove the skin from the ham (try to leave most of the fat in place). If desired, score the fat and stud with cloves. Place the meat on a rack in a roasting tin and pour in the wine.

Preheat the oven to 220°C, 425°F, Gas mark 7. Roast the meat for 30 minutes, then reduce the heat to 170°C, 325°F, Gas mark 3. Continue to cook, basting at frequent intervals with the wine. If this shows signs of drying up and catching, add a little water.

When the ham is done, remove to a warm serving plate to rest. Pour all the roasting juices into a bowl, allow the fat to rise and skim off as much as possible. Put about 2 tablespoons of the fat back into the roasting tin and sprinkle in a little flour. Stir well, and allow to cook gently for a few minutes. Then gradually stir in the juices, scraping well with a wooden spoon to incorporate any residue from the base and sides of the roasting tin. Bring to the boil and stir in some stock to make a lightly thickened gravy. Check for seasoning: it is unlikely that much, if any, salt will be needed, but some pepper is a good addition. Also, if the meat has been cooked plainly, a couple of cloves crushed to powder can be added at this stage, to give just a hint of spice.

Serve with roast or mashed potatoes and greens.

LEFTOVERS

British cookery traditions aren't strong on recipes for cold pork. The reasons are not obvious – perhaps it is to do with fresh pork being less ubiquitous than beef and mutton. Or perhaps it is simply that pork is pleasant to eat cold with salad and bread and needs little help. Certainly, pork is good with pickles and chutneys of the old-fashioned type, especially mustardy ones like piccalilli, which cut the fat.

Ham is another matter: it is more often eaten cold than hot. Ham salad has been a popular choice for a Sunday or other celebratory tea for 200 years, and the meat has probably been filling sandwiches for as long. Ham is also a useful ingredient in many other dishes, and can be used in combination with other meats in the following recipes: Chicken Sandwiches with Ravigote Butter (see page 112), Turkey Pie (see page 139) and Turkey Soup (see page 137).

'FRESH' PEA AND HAM SOUP

Stock from ham bones is traditionally used to make soup with dried peas – such as peas that have been stored for winter. There is nothing wrong with this and it can be very good; but we now tend to think of frozen rather than dried peas and these, too, make good soup.

SERVES 4

1 litre (1¾ pints) well-flavoured ham stock
500g (1lb 2oz) frozen garden peas
salt and pepper
a little cooked ham (optional)
chopped fresh parsley or coriander, to garnish

Put the stock on to heat and add the peas. Bring to the boil and cook gently for about 10 minutes, then blend to a purée (this will have a slightly rough texture).

Return to the pan and reheat, seasoning with salt and pepper to taste. If you have any leftover ham, cut it in small dice and add these too. Serve with a little chopped parsley or coriander in each bowl.

MUSTARD BUTTER FOR HAM SANDWICHES

The British – or at least, the English – have been making ham sandwiches for about 200 years, possibly longer. Mustard, usually of the pungent, bright yellow variety, was regarded as indispensable for these, at least for most of the 20th century. This is fine, but sometimes I prefer the Germanic tradition of mild, sweet mustard. Hence this flavoured butter.

MAKES 4–6

60g (2½oz) unsalted butter, softened
20g (¾oz) mild Dijon mustard
20g (¾oz) soft light brown sugar
1 dessertspoon lemon juice

Mix all the ingredients together thoroughly. Taste, and add more mustard, sugar or lemon juice if desired. Spread on slices of good sourdough bread, and top with layers of ham, cut as thinly as possible.

HASHED MEAT

SERVES 4

about 500g (1lb 2oz) cold roast pork or other
    meat, thinly sliced

FOR THE MARINADE
2 tablespoons leftover gravy or
    concentrated stock
1 tablespoon red wine vinegar
1 tablespoon redcurrant jelly
½ teaspoon salt
½ teaspoon ground black pepper
a little pounded mace
rosemary and a little sage
1 small onion, peeled and sliced in thin rings
a few celery leaves, chopped (optional)
1 tablespoon chopped parsley
1 tablespoon red wine or Marsala

FOR THE BROTH
125g (4½oz) onion, peeled
30g (1oz) celery
60g (2½oz) carrots
60g (2½oz) turnips
a small bunch of parsley
60g (2½oz) good dripping
600ml (1 pint) stock or water, heated
the trimmings and any bones from the roast

FOR THE SAUCE
30g (1oz) unsalted butter
30g (1oz) plain flour
salt and pepper

For the marinade, put the gravy in a small pan with 4 tablespoons hot water, then add the remaining ingredients. Warm gently, and as soon as the jelly has melted, remove from the heat. Cool and pour over the meat. Leave for up to 24 hours.

For the broth, finely chop the vegetables and parsley. Melt the dripping and add all the vegetables. Fry briskly, stirring frequently until they begin to brown at the edges. Add the hot stock plus any trimmings and bones from the roast. Simmer for about 1 hour with the lid ajar. Strain into a bowl and allow to cool. Lift off the surface fat.

Shortly before serving the hash, make the sauce. Melt the butter and stir in the flour. Cook gently for a few minutes, then gradually stir in the broth and bring to a simmer, stirring to make a smooth sauce. Lift the meat out of the marinade. Strain the latter and add the liquid to the sauce, stirring well and returning to boiling. Check the seasoning. Turn the heat low and lay in the slices of meat. Allow it to heat thoroughly (don't let the mixture boil, as it will toughen the meat), then serve.

PORK RISSOLES WITH SOUTH-EAST ASIAN SPICING

These rissoles are a kind of meatball. Medieval cooks used to make them using pork. Our ancestors would have added whatever seasonings they considered pleasing or fashionable at the time: ginger, nutmeg, lemon zest, anchovy, Worcestershire sauce. If lemongrass had been available, they would probably have used it; there are fashions in flavours just as in most other things.

MAKES 18–20

150g (5oz) cold roast pork, trimmed of skin, gristle and overcooked outside bits
50g (2oz) unsmoked bacon, without rind
2 mild green chilli peppers (or to taste), de-seeded
1 garlic clove, peeled
1 lemongrass stalk, trimmed of its outer layer
a small handful of green coriander sprigs
2 spring onions, trimmed and finely sliced
1 egg
½ teaspoon salt
oil or fat, for shallow frying

A NOTE ON FLAVOURINGS

The flavouring amounts given above are suggestions; alter them to taste. Chillies can vary in strength. Lemongrass can be a bit tired and stale – but if it lacks zing, be careful about adding too much, as it also has a woody, resistant texture, which can be unpleasant.

Cut the cold pork and the bacon into rough chunks, put into a food processor and process to a mixture with the texture of coarse breadcrumbs.

Roughly chop the chillies, garlic and lemongrass, and whizz them in a blender, together with the coriander, to a coarse paste. Stir into the meat, then add the spring onions, egg and salt, and mix to a paste.

Heat a little oil in a frying pan and drop in generous teaspoonfuls of the mixture to make flat little cakes. Fry briskly for a couple of minutes, then turn and fry until both sides are golden brown. Drain on kitchen paper.

If you prefer not to fry the rissoles, they can be dropped onto a lightly greased baking sheet and cooked in a preheated oven for about 10 minutes at 180°C, 350°F, Gas mark 4. Turn once halfway through cooking. Serve the rissoles with salad.

RISSOLES WITH PARMESAN PASTRY

Another recipe poached from Colonel Kenney-Herbert (see page 60). Worth taking pains over, these little deep-fried pastries make delicious morsels. The Edwardians might have eaten them at lunch or piled them up as a side dish for dinner; I like them as a nibble with drinks.

MAKES 18–24

250g (9oz) cold roast lean meat, trimmed
    of skin and gristle
leftover gravy (or use broth, see page 86)
salt and pepper
vegetable oil, for deep frying

FOR THE PASTRY
100g (4oz) plain flour, plus extra for dusting
1 large egg, separated
50g (2oz) unsalted butter, softened
50g (2oz) Parmesan, finely grated
1–2 tablespoons water

To make the pastry, put the flour in a bowl or on a slab, make a hollow and drop the egg yolk in. Add the butter and Parmesan and work with your fingertips to form a paste. Add a little water and work to a smooth, soft dough. Cover and leave to rest.

Mince the cold meat finely; use a knife so that a little texture is retained. Mix with a few tablespoons of gravy to give a mixture that is moist but not runny. Add seasoning to taste.

Dust a work surface with flour and roll the pastry out thinly (about the thickness of a twopence piece). Cut out circles with a diameter of 7cm (2¾in). Heap 1 generous teaspoon of filling on one side of each circle. Brush the edge of the pastry with a little egg white, then fold each circle of pastry in half to enclose the filling. Press the edges together gently to make shapes like tiny Cornish pasties, and give them a few minutes to firm.

Heat the oil in a deep-fat fryer to 180°C, 350°F and fry until golden brown. Remove with a slotted spoon, drain on kitchen paper and serve immediately. If you prefer, the rissoles can be baked for 10 minutes at 180°C, 350°F, Gas mark 4.

POTTED HAM

A good method for using up cold ham. Potting started off with raw meat cooked specifically for the purpose (it was a means of preserving, on a similar principle to French confit de canard*). Over the years, the recipes changed and became lighter and softer (and eventually evolved into the various 'pastes' sold as sandwich fillings).*

SERVES 4

250g (9oz) cold cooked ham
freshly ground black pepper
ground mace, allspice or star anise
125g (4½oz) unsalted butter, softened

Take a piece of cold ham and remove any gristly bits, skin and connective tissue, and any outside edges that have hardened and browned in cooking (these can all go in the stockpot). Fat (unless there is an excessive amount) can be incorporated into the potting process. Cut the ham into small chunks and then blitz it in a food processor. Add some black pepper and your other chosen seasonings. Mace and allspice are traditional; star anise isn't, but a suspicion, finely pounded, is good. Don't overdo the seasoning, and if you choose to add star anise, don't mix it with any other spices but pepper, and add a very small pinch, otherwise it will be overpowering.

Beat the softened butter until creamy and mix in the seasoned ham. Put the mixture into a serving dish, such as a china soufflé dish, then chill. Serve for lunch or tea, with hot toast or good bread.

Chicken, Guinea Fowl & Quail

Together with turkeys, ducks and geese, these birds are classified as poultry – domestic birds reared for the table. With the exception of quail (which were always wild birds until the development of quail farming in the second half of the 20th century), these were small, adaptable farmyard scavengers. They were often seasonal, and were sought after as delicacies at particular times of the year, but as domestic birds they had less status than game, and were more accessible to the general population. Chickens, especially, could be kept in very small spaces. We buy chickens all year round, expecting them to be tender and varying in price according to weight, along with other factors relating to the way in which they are produced. Our ancestors priced chickens differently – by age and time of year. In 1845, Eliza Acton wrote:

Fowls are always in season when they can be procured sufficiently young to be tender. About February they become dear and scarce; and small spring chickens are generally very expensive. As summer advances they decline in price.

This relates directly back to the cycle of egg-laying and hatching, which was at its lowest point in mid-winter, but increased dramatically as soon as the days began to lengthen. The majority of birds hatched around Easter, flooded the market and the price came down as summer went on. They grew much more slowly than modern commercial stock – whose swift growth rate would have seemed extraordinary to farmers in the past.

A spring chicken really was a spring chicken – hatched in mid- to late winter, and ready for the table as a luxury in spring. It was simply roasted and appreciated for its tender flesh and delicate flavour. Smaller birds, the equivalent of poussins, were available, and were often grilled; older fowls were also plentiful, but were more suitable for boiling. Capons (castrated cockerels) were also once much esteemed, as they grew to be large, fat table birds.

Generally, we favoured young tender chickens – and that is what we now get, but at the price of compromising production systems, with repercussions for the welfare of the live birds, and a loss of flavour. It is difficult now to imagine what a luxury a roast chicken was right up until the 1960s.

Domestic chickens have come a very long way from their probable origin as wild south-east Asian jungle fowl that were slowly domesticated and gradually spread westwards, arriving in the British Isles shortly before the Roman conquest. From then, they scratched around farmyards, dunghills and urban backyards, probably with little change over the centuries – until, like all other farm animals, they began to receive the attention of agricultural improvers in the 18th and 19th centuries. They were improved by an input from Asian strains, which caused quite a stir because of their often very decorative appearance. The process by which the changes happened is largely unrecorded, because poultry breeding was generally a hobby for the urban working class, especially in the north of England. That said, many ladies – including Queen Victoria herself – kept fancy poultry as ornamental birds.

The counties around London, especially Surrey, Kent and Sussex, specialised in producing fat chickens for the London market, which showed a preference for white-fleshed birds. In the late 19th century, the creatures were crammed with oatmeal to give a fine flavour and texture. The ideal table fowl was required to have lots of tender white breast meat and light bones; economics, as always, looked for a bird that was early maturing. 'Sussex' breeds of hen developed from this demand, and the characteristics can still

be detected in birds reared for the broiler system developed in the 1950s. The most common commercial breeds are Ross and Cobb, bred to be reared in a controlled indoor environment, gain weight very quickly and provide large amounts of white meat.

At tables in the past, a plain roast chicken with bread sauce and some type of stuffing was considered fine material for a Sunday lunch, and in the 18th century was served as a delicacy as part of a larger meal of multiple dishes. The traditional accompaniment of bread sauce dates back to the Middle Ages, when breadcrumbs were used to thicken and bind spiced sauces. The use of other flavours and sauces with chicken followed the general trends over the centuries, but the British seem to have developed dishes using large amounts of pungent aromatics such as tarragon or garlic under French influence.

Roast chicken is excellent cold, and was a good dish for a ball supper (especially with mayonnaise and salad), or for a picnic (an event much enjoyed by the English, despite the weather, and one that was a feature of 19th-century social life). The meat could be made into many other dishes, and the bones produce good stock – so they were always sought after.

Guinea Fowl and Quail

Neither of these birds is related to chickens, but both are farmed for their meat in Britain.

Guinea fowl are indigenous to Africa; known in parts of the Mediterranean by Classical times, they became more widespread in early modern times through links between Guinea and Portugal (hence the English name). The live birds have attractive spotted plumage and a rounded, bustling shape. They have been used in British cookery since the 16th century or before, but there are few specific recipes for them.

As wild birds, European quail are often summer visitors to south-eastern Britain. The farmed birds are a domesticated variety, Japanese quail, which are usually very small and delicately flavoured.

Buying and Preparation

As a child, I was privileged to live on a farm with ample opportunity to observe some (very) free-range hens. My favourite source now is a local farm shop run by a woman who takes enormous pride in her poultry flock, and an equal pride in their presentation – plump, properly plucked, nicely trussed, complete with giblets. The flavour is excellent. If buying in a supermarket, look at the quality symbols and aim for one that ensures the optimum in terms of space and access to outdoors. The ability to range freely and a diet rich in grain both make a difference to the flavour.

Quality labels can help in making a choice. Label Rouge (Red Label) birds are slower-growing breeds reared in France under certified, pasture-based conditions with the best flavour in mind. They will be expensive. Supermarkets often have their own premium ranges, which make claims about welfare and feed. Individual producers (who mostly sell via their own shops and networks, or online) often give a lot of detail about the conditions under which their birds are reared. Transparency in labelling, and in both supplier and producer, are all-important with chicken and poultry in general. The more anonymous a product, the less likely it is to have been treated with care at any stage.

Guinea fowl and quail also suffer from intensive rearing. It is difficult to know exactly what system has been used; generally you should assume this will have been intensive, unless stated otherwise. Both these birds are often imported, from unknown welfare systems abroad.

When buying chicken, a poussin is a very small young bird, weighing 450–500g (1lb–1lb 2oz), which will feed one person.

A chicken – an older bird, though perhaps no more than 6–8 weeks old – will weigh around 1.5kg (3½lb) and feed 4 people. Older, larger birds – up to about 2.5kg (5½lb), and sometimes bigger – will feed up to 6 people.

Guinea-fowl meat is similar to that of a good free-range chicken but is leaner and gamier in flavour. The birds are also smaller than chickens, and generally weigh 1–1.5kg (2¼lb–3½lb). One bird will serve 3–4 people. For quail, allow 1–2 birds per person.

The less a chicken costs, the more likely it is to need attention when it arrives in the kitchen. Remove and discard all wrappings and any elastic bands used to truss the bird (if it is trussed with string stitched through from side to side, the chances are that it has been properly prepared, and you won't need to do much). Pluck out any stubs and bits of feather. Dry the skin with kitchen paper, and dry the inside of the bird as well. Remove any obvious bits of pipe and trim the skin of the neck neatly.

Chickens, and most other birds, used to arrive with a little package of giblets – the neck, heart, gizzard and liver. Use these, if there are any, to make stock (see right). Very few chickens seem to come with giblets now.

The purpose of trussing a chicken during cooking is to make it look neat, compact and well shaped; to keep it tidy without any projecting bits to scorch (especially important for spit-roasting), ultimately giving a plump-looking bird which would present well at table. In practice, when roasting birds in the oven, I find that a trussed bird tends to be undercooked between the thigh and body when the rest of the bird is done. For this reason, I tend to remove ties about two-thirds of the way through cooking.

Chicken Giblet Stock

Should you manage to acquire a chicken with giblets, check the liver carefully to make sure the bitter-tasting dark green gall bladder has been discarded. Add the liver to a stuffing, pâté or a ragù for pasta.

Put the remaining giblets in a small pan with a bay leaf, a few parsley stalks and a few pieces of onion, carrot and celery if available, cover with water and bring to the boil. Skim, then cover and leave to simmer gently for about an hour. Top up with more water if necessary. Strain, discarding the debris and reserve the stock for gravy.

Roasting Times

Chicken must always be well cooked. Underdone, it is a notorious source of food poisoning. Because of this, it is better not to stuff the body cavity of the bird, as the heat may not reach the centre of the stuffing by the time the meat is done. Cook the stuffing in a separate dish. Occasionally a thin layer of stuffing or flavouring is spread between the skin and the meat of the breast (see Roast Pullet with Gammon, page 104), a method that adds flavour and fat to the meat underneath.

Chicken is sometimes served with little sausages and bacon as well as bread sauce, or barded with bacon like game birds. If you don't bard it, protect the breast with buttered paper or tinfoil during the early stages of cooking.

Standard instructions for roasting a chicken are to start it off at 200°C, 400°F, Gas mark 6 for 20 minutes, then reduce the heat to 180°C, 350°F, Gas mark 4 and cook for 20–25 minutes per 500g until the juices run clear. Examine the meat between the leg and the body; if any hint of pink shows here, or in the juices that flow from the thickest part of the thigh when pierced with a skewer, the bird needs further cooking. If you have a probe thermometer, measure the temperature of the thickest part of the thigh (but not touching the bone): it should be at least 70°C (160°F). Allow for resting after cooking time.

For guinea fowl and quail, see recipes on pages 107 and 109.

Basic Roast Chicken

A classic roast chicken is a firm favourite for Sunday lunch. When cooked with care, roast chicken boasts a crispy, tasty skin and juicy, succulent flesh. The cold leftovers lend themselves to myriad salads, sandwiches and other dishes.

SERVES 4–5

½ lemon
1 chicken, weighing 2kg (4½lb)
a few sprigs of fresh herbs,
    such as parsley, thyme or
    marjoram (optional)
2 unsmoked bacon rashers
    (optional)
unsalted butter
3–4 tablespoons white wine
    or water
½ teaspoon salt
Chicken Giblet Stock
    (see page 96) or other
    chicken stock
scant 1 tablespoon plain flour
freshly ground black pepper

Preheat the oven to 200°C, 400°F, Gas mark 6. Put the lemon (which could be one you've squeezed all the juice out of) into the body cavity of the bird, along with the herbs. Bard the breast with bacon if you wish, or spread a little butter on it. Also spread a little butter over the roasting tin (just enough to stop the bird sticking as it starts to cook), and put the bird in. Calculate the roasting time (see page 97).

It's often better to start roasting a chicken on its side, especially if it is a large bird and your oven is an unreliable gas one like mine. Cover with a lid if the tin has one, or with a piece of oiled or buttered foil. Roast for about 20 minutes, then reduce the heat to 180°C, 350°F, Gas mark 4. After another 10 minutes, turn the bird onto the other side; cover and roast for another 15–20 minutes, then turn it onto its back. Add the white wine or water, cover, and return to the oven for another 30 minutes.

Remove the foil, then baste the bird well with the cooking juices and sprinkle the salt over the skin. Return, uncovered, to the oven for the remainder of the roasting time. Check every 10 minutes or so to make sure the juices aren't burning (a good chestnut brown is OK; black definitely isn't). If they show signs of overcooking, add a little water. The skin should crisp and brown nicely. Baste once or twice more with the cooking juices – this helps to produce a really crisp, tasty skin.

The bird is done when the juices from the thickest part of the leg run clear (pierce it with a clean skewer or the tip of a sharp knife). Make sure the meat around the hip joint between the leg and the body is fully done; there should be no trace of pink. If there is, return the bird to the oven for a few minutes.

When it is fully cooked, remove it from the roasting tin to a warm serving plate while you make the gravy. Pour all the juices into a bowl, deglaze the tin with a little stock and add the result to the rest of the juices. Return the tin to the heat, then add a couple of tablespoons of the fat that will have risen to the top of the cooking juices and stir in the flour, allowing it to cook gently and turn a nutty brown. Remove as much fat as possible from the remaining juice and then stir gradually into the mixture in the roasting tin. Stir in the giblet stock, taste and adjust the seasoning.

Roast Chicken with Orange and Lemon

Citrus fruits were favourite flavourings for all sorts of meat dishes by the late 16th century, when they were used in combination with sweet spices and dried fruit. This recipe uses orange and lemon only, producing a very intense, slightly sharp-flavoured gravy.

SERVES 4–5

1 chicken, weighing 2kg (4½lb)
salt and pepper
juice and pared zest of
    1 lemon (preferably
    unwaxed)
juice and pared zest of
    1 orange (preferably
    unwaxed)
a few sprigs of fresh herbs,
    such as parsley, thyme or
    marjoram (optional)
splash of stock, to deglaze

Start the chicken off as in the basic method (see page 98). When you turn the chicken onto its back, pour the fruit juices over. Cover again and return to the oven. About 30 minutes before the end of cooking time, uncover, baste, then salt the skin and add the zest, cut in thin strips, to the juices and return to the oven. Baste again a couple more times. Take special care to watch that the juices in the tin don't burn; add extra stock or water if necessary.

At the end of cooking time, the bird should have a deep gold-brown and very crisp skin. (Turn the oven up to 220°C, 425°F, Gas mark 7 for a few minutes to get it really brown and crisp at the end, if necessary, but do watch for burning.) There should be a relatively small amount of juice with a very concentrated flavour in the roasting tin. Pour off the juices and deglaze the tin with a little stock. Skim the fat off the juices and add the deglazed cooking residue, but don't attempt to make a thickened gravy – just give everyone a spoonful or two of the cooking juices with the meat.

Roast Chicken with Tarragon

The fresh, grassy, slightly aniseed note of tarragon is a classic partner for chicken in French cookery, with many variations on the theme, using poached or roast chicken, served hot or cold. Although recipes for the dish have appeared in several English cookery books over the last 100 years or so, it never seems to have become really popular, perhaps because French tarragon is not especially easy to grow in Britain (Russian tarragon, much more vigorous, lacks the flavour of the French variety). This is based on a recipe given by Elizabeth David in Summer Cooking *(1965).*

MAKES 4–5

a small bunch of fresh
    tarragon
60g (2½oz) unsalted butter
1 chicken, weighing 2kg (4½lb)
1 teaspoon grated lemon zest
    (preferably unwaxed), plus
    ½ the lemon
salt and pepper
100ml (3½fl oz) white wine
    or chicken stock
generous 1 teaspoon
    plain flour
150ml (5fl oz) single cream

Pick the leaves off the tarragon and chop them. Mix a generous tablespoonful of chopped leaves with most of the butter – leave about 15g (½oz) for finishing the sauce. Put the tarragon butter, and the ½ lemon, inside the bird. Roast as in the basic method given on page 98, basting from time to time with the cooking juices, turning it onto its back after 45 minutes, and seasoning with salt and pepper towards the end of cooking.

When the bird is cooked, remove it to a warmed plate and pour all the juices into a bowl. Deglaze the tin with the white wine, making sure it bubbles fiercely, or with a little chicken stock. Add all the herby, buttery juices back into the roasting tin. Add the lemon zest and the remaining butter worked together with the flour. Stir well, then add the cream and the rest of the chopped tarragon, and heat until the sauce boils and thickens.

Roast Pullet with Gammon

The inspiration for this recipe came from John Nott in The Cook's and Confectioner's Dictionary *(1723). His recipes reflect the rich, meaty dishes popular among the aristocracy of the early 18th century. A pullet – a young laying hen – was an especially prodigal use of resources.*

SERVES 4

100g (4oz) lean gammon
    (or unsmoked bacon,
    fat removed)
2 tablespoons finely chopped
    fresh herbs – a mixture of
    parsley, chives and basil
salt and pepper
1 chicken, on the small side –
    about 1.5kg (3½lb)
olive oil or unsalted butter
splash of chicken stock

Preheat the oven to 180°C, 350°F, Gas mark 4. Mince the gammon. In an 18th-century kitchen, some unfortunate maid or scullion would have had to do this on a board with two knives; for us, a food processor works very well. Mix the minced meat with the chopped herbs, then season; go easy on the salt, as the gammon will already be salty, but be fairly generous with the pepper.

Carefully ease the skin away from the flesh over the breast of the chicken. Divide the gammon and herb mixture in two and spread it over each side of the bird, between the meat of the breast and the skin. Pull the skin back and sew or skewer it at the neck so that the stuffing remains in place during cooking.

Spread a little olive oil or butter in a roasting tin and put the bird in. Cover the breast with a piece of tinfoil, as the skin cooks through quickly in this recipe. (Start the bird off breast down if this works better in your oven, but when you turn it onto its back, use a piece of tinfoil to protect the breast until cooking is nearly completed.) Calculate the cooking time (see page 97) and roast until the bird is three-quarters cooked. Then remove the foil, baste well, sprinkle the bird with salt and continue roasting until fully cooked.

Put the bird on a warmed platter to rest, removing any strings or skewers. Skim the fat off the cooking juices and deglaze with a little stock. Check the seasoning and serve.

CHICKEN, GUINEA FOWL & QUAIL

105

Roast Guinea Fowl

Recipes for roasting guinea fowl – or guinea-hens, as they were sometimes called – appear from the 19th century onwards; the English usually seem to have treated the birds simply, regarding them in the same light as pheasants. They can be tricky to cook well, as the meat on the breast tends to cook through and dry out before the legs are fully cooked. Turning the bird during cooking can help to overcome this to some extent.

SERVES 3–4

unsalted butter
2–4 rashers unsmoked
    streaky bacon
1 guinea fowl, about 1kg (2¼lb)
salt and pepper
100ml (3½fl oz) port (optional)
150ml (5fl oz) well-flavoured
    chicken stock

Lightly butter a small roasting tin in which the guinea fowl will fit nicely. Wrap the bacon around the breast of the bird and tie on with string.

Preheat the oven to 200°C, 400°F, Gas mark 6. Roast the bird for 20 minutes at this temperature, then reduce the heat to 180°C, 350°F, Gas mark 4 and cook for a further 25 minutes. Then remove the bacon, season with a little salt and continue to roast until the juices run clear. Allow to rest for about 10 minutes before serving.

To make the gravy, pour off all the cooking juices into a bowl and skim off and discard the fat that rises to the surface. Deglaze the roasting dish with the port, if using, or the chicken stock. Add the cooking juices and boil hard to produce a fairly small amount of thin, well-flavoured gravy. Adjust the seasoning with salt and pepper as necessary.

To accompany a guinea fowl, serve Bread Sauce (page 190) or Cashew Nut Sauce (page 108). A Wild Rice Pilaf is very good with this (page 108). A salad of watercress was favoured as an accompaniment by 19th-century cookery authors, but, writing in 1905, Colonel Kenney-Herbert suggested a salad of cos lettuce dressed with wine vinegar, oil, and a seasoning of 1 teaspoon each of chopped tarragon and chives.

Wild Rice Pilaf

SERVES 3–4

20g (¾oz) dried chanterelles
125–150g (4½–5oz) wild rice
20g (¾oz) unsalted butter
1 medium onion, peeled and
    finely chopped
150–200g (5–7oz) chestnut
    mushrooms, trimmed
    and sliced
salt and pepper
50g (2oz) almonds, blanched
    and cut into slivers
1–2 tablespoons parsley,
    finely chopped

Rinse the dried chanterelles and put in a small bowl; cover with boiling water and leave to soak. Put the wild rice in a pan and cover generously with boiling water; simmer gently until cooked, about 45 minutes. Melt the butter in a large frying pan and cook the onion gently, stirring from time to time until the pieces begin to turn a pale gold. Add the chestnut mushrooms and continue to cook gently, stirring occasionally until all the liquid they exude has evaporated.

When the wild rice is cooked, drain and stir into the onion-mushroom mixture. Drain the chanterelles and add these too. Check the seasoning and adjust as necessary. Toast the almonds for 5–10 minutes. Stir these and the chopped parsley through the wild rice mixture just before serving.

Cashew Nut Sauce

SERVES 3–4

40g (1½oz) unsalted butter
¼ small onion, peeled and
    very finely chopped
75g (3oz) raw cashew nuts
roux made with 15g (½oz)
    plain flour and 15g (½oz)
    unsalted butter
150ml (5fl oz) chicken or
    game stock
salt and pepper

Melt the butter in a small frying pan, add the onion and the cashew nuts, and fry gently until the nuts become pale gold in colour. Empty the mixture into a food processor and whizz to a paste.

Use a small pan to make the roux, and once it is smooth and has cooked for a few minutes, stir in the nut paste plus enough stock to make a sauce. Season to taste and serve.

Roast Quail with Vine Leaves and Grapes

In the UK, quail are almost always farmed, and generally very small. They are best quite plainly cooked, and the standard instruction in English cookery books of previous centuries was always to wrap them in vine leaves. This is a nice idea, if you can beg or steal some fresh leaves from someone, although I'm not convinced it makes a great difference to the flavour.

SERVES 4

8 quail
salt and pepper
a handful of small white
    seedless grapes
8 large vine leaves, if available
8 rashers unsmoked streaky
    bacon, thinly cut, or
    unsmoked pancetta
unsalted butter, melted
100ml (3½fl oz) white wine

Preheat the oven to 200°C, 400°F, Gas mark 6.

Season each bird with salt and pepper and pop a couple of grapes inside. Fold each bird in a vine leaf, then wrap a piece of bacon around it and tie in place with string. Brush each one with a little melted butter. Arrange the quail in a shallow roasting tin and pour over the white wine. Roast for 20–25 minutes, basting a couple of times with the wine and buttery juices.

Serve the quail still wrapped in their vine-leaf parcels, with the cooking juices, skimmed of fat. Game Chips (see page 169) go well with quail, and a green salad tastes better with quail than cooked vegetables.

LEFTOVERS

A good roast chicken is delicious cold as well as hot. Accompaniments can be very simple – some good bread, a well-made salad and a bottle of chilled white wine make it into a meal. Some more elaborate cold chicken dishes became classics of the English kitchen. Although the recipes are for whole chickens, they can easily be scaled down to cope with the remains of a bird already partly carved for a previous meal.

JULIENNE SOUP

'Julienne' vegetables (cut into long narrow strips) were often used in soups in late 19th-century Britain. This is a typical mix, giving a light, fresh summery soup for a day when you have a well-flavoured chicken stock to use.

SERVES 4

125g (4½oz) carrot

40g (1½oz) turnip

125g (4½oz) celery

200g (7oz) asparagus

125g (4½oz) onion, peeled

40g (1½oz) unsalted butter

about 1 teaspoon chopped fresh tarragon

1 litre (1¾ pints) well-flavoured chicken stock

1 small lettuce

½ teaspoon granulated sugar

salt

a little chopped fresh parsley

finely grated Parmesan, to serve

Cut the carrot, turnip, celery and asparagus stems into batons about 2cm (¾in) long and 5mm (¼in) square (the asparagus tips can be left whole and reserved until the end of cooking). Slice the onion into fine slivers.

Melt the butter in a large saucepan. Add the vegetables and the tarragon, cover tightly, and cook over low heat for 15–20 minutes, stirring from time to time. Then add the chicken stock and simmer for about 10 minutes. At the end of this time, add the asparagus tips and the lettuce, cut into thin strips. Cook for 5–10 minutes longer. Add the sugar, and salt as you feel necessary. Ladle into soup bowls and garnish with chopped parsley. Hand the Parmesan cheese separately.

MAYONNAISE OF FOWL

This is the name Mrs de Salis gave in Sweets and Supper Dishes à la Mode *(1895). In typically late Victorian style, it was heavily decorated: she says 'garnish round the base with a border of hard-boiled eggs cut in quarters, olives, fillets of anchovies, and chopped aspic; ornament the top with a few sprigs of tarragon and chopped aspic.' Aspic was a favourite garnish of 19th-century cooks, and would probably now be dispensed with, but a garnish of eggs, olives, anchovies and tarragon provides an excellent foil for the gentler flavours of the chicken and the mayonnaise.*

SERVES 4–6

1 cold roast chicken

3 tablespoons olive oil

1 tablespoon wine vinegar

salt and pepper

lettuce (inner leaves from soft, flat lettuces,
     or use lamb's lettuce)

mayonnaise

tarragon, chervil or parsley, to decorate

Joint the chicken, separating the drumsticks from the thighs. Cut off the wings and divide into joints. Cut the breast meat into neat pieces. Mix the oil, vinegar, a little salt and pepper, and marinate the chicken for 1–2 hours.

Make a bed of lettuce on a serving dish. Drain the chicken from the vinaigrette and arrange on the lettuce. Use mayonnaise to mask the chicken and decorate with the herbs. Serve immediately.

VARIATIONS
Mrs de Salis assumed that the cook would know how to produce mayonnaise of the right consistency. Out of expediency or nervousness about raw eggs, we'd probably reach for bottled mayonnaise, which is fine as long as it's a good one. Slacken the consistency with a little tepid water, or mix with a little natural yoghurt.

CHICKEN SANDWICHES
WITH RAVIGOTE BUTTER

An idea from Colonel Kenney-Herbert's Common-Sense Cookery *(1905), given in a short section on sandwiches. Ravigote butter is not well known in the modern kitchen, but it is delicious and useful for all sorts of sandwiches. The name is derived from the French verb* ravigoter, *'to perk up'.*

Burnet, a salad herb of long-established meadows, has pretty oval leaves with serrated edges. Its flavour is reminiscent of cucumbers. It is not usually seen on sale, but can easily be grown in a pot or a sunny corner. If it is unobtainable, either omit it, or replace it with parsley, which gives the classic French fines herbes *combination. This recipe makes quite a large amount but it can be frozen, or used with other dishes – with plain roast chicken or eggs, for instance. The recipe works equally well with turkey or ham.*

MAKES 12

leftover meat from 1 cold roast chicken (or
    turkey or ham), chopped into julienne strips

FOR THE RAVIGOTE BUTTER
30g (1oz) fresh chervil
30g (1oz) fresh tarragon
30g (1oz) fresh chives
30g (1oz) fresh burnet (optional)
250g (9oz) unsalted butter, softened

Pick over the herbs and wash them, then scald by placing in a small bowl and pouring boiling water over them. Leave for 2 minutes. Drain on kitchen paper, then put them in a blender and chop as finely as possible. Add the butter gradually, to achieve a paste that is as smooth as possible.

For sandwiches, use equal quantities of chicken, turkey or ham (the Colonel suggests also using tongue or foie gras, similarly cut). Sandwich them between day-old slices of bread, thinly cut and spread with ravigote butter.

Half the suggested amount of herbs and butter is about right for 12 slices of average-sized sandwich bread. Because the chicken is cut into small strips, it doesn't matter if the less glamorously shaped pickings off the carcass are used.

CORONATION CHICKEN

Devised for the coronation of Queen Elizabeth II in 1953, this could be regarded as a variation on the theme of chicken mayonnaise. The industrial versions used as sandwich fillings in the 1990s did few favours for what is, when well made, a delicious dish, which most people love.

SERVES 4–6

2 tablespoons sunflower oil

1 small onion, peeled and very finely chopped

1 dessertspoon curry powder (mild Madras)

generous 1 tablespoon mango chutney, rubbed through a sieve

250g (9oz) mayonnaise (home-made or good-quality bottled)

salt and pepper

1 cold roast chicken, skinned, boned and divided into neat, roughly bite-sized chunks

flaked almonds, toasted until golden brown

lettuce leaves, lightly dressed with oil and vinegar, to serve

Heat the oil and fry the onion very gently until translucent. Stir in the curry powder and continue to cook gently until it loses its raw smell. Remove from the heat and allow to cool.

Stir in the mango chutney and the mayonnaise to make a thick, lightly curried cold sauce. Taste and adjust the seasoning. Arrange the chicken pieces on top of the lettuce leaves and pour the curried mayonnaise over. Scatter the almonds on top.

Turkey,
Goose &
Duck

Like other poultry, turkeys, geese and ducks have long been reared for British dinner tables, especially for special occasions like Christmas.

Turkey

In Britain, it's difficult to think of turkey without thinking of Christmas. When these birds first arrived, shortly after European explorers discovered the Americas, they were an exotic curiosity. However, they fitted into a recognisable place in the eating habits of the time – as a large bird among the many already served at the tables of the rich at great feasts and important occasions. Christmas was undoubtedly one of these; the association between the two developed early on. Prices for turkeys were cited in London markets by the 1550s, when they were also mentioned in conjunction with Christmas by Thomas Tusser. By the 17th century, turkeys had spread across England – partly because they were novelties, albeit difficult ones (they detest wet conditions). Rearing turkeys became a speciality of East Anglia, especially Norfolk, in the 17th and 18th centuries. The birds were turned loose on the stubble after harvest to fatten on any stray corn, and were then driven, on foot, to the Christmas markets of large towns and to London.

Like chickens, turkeys were seasonal to some extent. Turkey poults (young birds) were very expensive in early spring, but prices dropped as the summer wore on, and into the autumn. But even in the first half of the 19th century, demand was by far the strongest in mid-December. Eliza Acton remarked 'The great demand for turkeys in England towards Christmas, and the care which they require in being reared, causes them to be brought much less abundantly into the markets when young, than they are in foreign countries; in many of which they are very plentiful and very cheap.'

Roasting a turkey in the past was obviously regarded as almost as much of an undertaking as it is now. Suggested spit-roasting times are relatively short by our standards. However, cooks were always entreated to make sure that the bird was fully done, preferably by allowing it time to come to room temperature before roasting – a reflection of the fact that the birds were mostly cooked in winter, and that old-fashioned larders were chilly. Another point noted by cookery writers in the past was that the sinews in a turkey's legs should be pulled (large birds develop tough sinews to keep them upright), and that doing so could be difficult. In her *Practical Cookery Book* (1898) Mrs Roundell suggested shutting the bird's legs in the crack of a door, with one person inside holding the bird, and the other outside, pulling on the legs. We may be squeamish about such things, but a cook in a good household would have to know how to carry out such procedures in order to serve a bird that was considered properly dressed.

Turkeys were trussed like chicken for roasting, the wings and legs tied close to the body, sometimes with the gizzard of the bird under one wing, and its liver under the other. This English mode exasperated the French chef Alexis Soyer, who in 1849 considered that treating the liver this way would spoil the look of the bird once roasted (because it would drip juices down the side as it cooked), but the 'liver-wing' was considered a delicacy until the mid-19th century.

Stuffings of various descriptions were almost always used with turkeys by the 18th century, mostly in the crop (at the front of the breast). A standard English type of stuffing with herbs and lemon was one option; other mixtures used cooked veal, pork sausagemeat or chestnuts. Pork products of various kinds, including sausages, have been consistently used with turkeys over the centuries. For an elaborate dish, the bird could be made into a galantine by boning it, filling with stuffing and sewing it up again before cooking. Hannah Glasse, in *The Art of*

Cookery Made Plain and Easy, published in 1747, gave an early recipe for this under the title 'To roast a turky the genteel way', using a highly seasoned stuffing based on veal or chicken. More usually wrapped in a cloth and simmered in water, this is a good way of dealing with a small bird.

The idea of a turkey as a special feast remains, despite intensive production. Acquire a well-produced bird and cook it gently (the recipe on page 124 is a revelation), and think about the feasts of fowl – wild and domestic – enjoyed in the houses of the Elizabethan nobility.

Goose

Christmas is coming, the geese are getting fat ... Domestic geese are probably descended from wild geese native to Europe. Even the rural poor could keep a few, pastured on common land, and for many centuries they were Christmas food. It was a goose that Ebenezer Scrooge bought for the Cratchit family in Charles Dickens' *A Christmas Carol* (1843), but a century later turkeys had supplanted them on the festive table.

Geese are resistant to attempts to farm them intensively. They need space and grass to graze on, and they remain highly seasonal as food. Until the 19th century, geese were eaten during the autumn as well as at Christmas. Like most birds, the young hatched in spring were at their peak in autumn, still tender, and fat because they had had all summer to feed. A stubble-fattened goose was a traditional item for a Michaelmas dinner – 29th September was an important date because it was one of the 'quarter' days of the English calendar, when rents and debts were paid. This was the start of the season when geese were at their best, which ran through until Christmas. Young birds were also eaten as 'green geese' around Whitsuntide, served with sorrel sauce, but never stuffed.

In the middle of the 20th century, goose became difficult to buy as the poultry industry intensified. Turkey became the norm, and the small mixed farms that used to rear a few geese every year became uneconomic. Interest in geese has revived recently, partly because they have a deep, rich flavour, quite different from turkey, and partly because of their resistance to intensive systems.

In the past, geese were cooked by a variety of methods, but roasting was always a favourite because it both removes the copious fat and produces a delicious crisp skin. Carving a goose was something of a ceremony in the 19th century. The carver started by cutting away the 'apron', the skin below the breast, and pouring a glass of claret mixed with mustard into the bird, before removing some of the stuffing. A 'graceful and well-skilled' carver reckoned never to have to turn a bird on its side to disjoint the leg, but it was acknowledged that this was sometimes a necessity when carving goose, as the hip sockets are difficult to reach with the carving knife.

Sage and onion stuffing seems to have been the invariable accompaniment – to the extent that some cuts of other meats cooked with it were sometimes called 'mock goose'. Cooks always differed about how apparent the flavourings should be. In 1747, Hannah Glasse warned 'never put Onion into any thing unless you are sure every body loves it'. Colonel Kenney-Herbert and Mrs Roundell, in the late 19th century, both appear to have considered sage objectionably strong, and subdued its flavour by blanching. Potato stuffings for goose, with apple, onion, shallot or herbs, are mentioned in several mid-19th-century cookery books, and some variation on this is an excellent idea.

Goose Giblet Stock

Heat a little unsalted butter in a saucepan, add the giblets of the bird and 2–3 rashers of chopped, unsmoked bacon. Chop one small carrot, ½ an onion and ½ a celery stick and add to the pan. Cook briskly, stirring frequently, until beginning to brown. Pour in 100ml red wine or 2–3 tablespoons Madeira, and cook until reduced by half. Add a bouquet garni of fresh thyme, parsley and marjoram and 400ml chicken stock. Bring to a simmer and cook gently for 1 hour. Strain and skim off any fat.

Duck

European domestic ducks are probably descended from mallards, the typical wild ducks of the British countryside, the drakes with dark iridescent heads, the female ducks speckled mid-brown. Like geese, domestic ducks were often reared by smallholders, the birds congregating around farm or village pond. For more than 100 years, from the first part of 19th century until the 1920s, Aylesbury in Buckinghamshire was the name associated with ducks for the table in Britain. This breed, large and white-feathered, was raised, according to Isabella Beeton:

> … in the abodes of the cottagers. Round the walls of the living-rooms, and of the bedroom even, are fixed rows of wooden boxes, lined with hay; and it is the business of the wife and children to nurse and comfort the feathered lodgers, to feed the little ducklings, and to take the old ones out for an airing.

The system was similar to one of share-cropping, with the stock being provided by a wealthier partner in the business. As ever, their reputation in London played a part in their fame, Smithfield Market being easily accessible from Buckinghamshire from the mid-19th century onwards.

By World War I, hybrid ducks with Chinese blood were common, and providing competition for the Aylesbury. Subsequently, duck farming was subject to the same pressures towards intensification as chicken and turkey production, with high stocking densities, and no access to water for swimming, which is an essential part of duck behaviour. Until duck farming made ducks available all year round, ducklings (half-grown birds) filled a gap in the calendar in spring, when poultry generally was scarce and the game season had come to an end.

The combination of duck with orange appears quite early on, with orange juice being mentioned as a sauce or flavouring for teal (small wild duck) in the mid-17th century by the French cook, La Varenne. The fruit has been used consistently with duck, both wild and tame, up to the present day. Fashions in more savoury flavours have varied, with typically meaty, savoury combinations in the 18th century; olives were sometimes suggested for flavouring sauces in the 19th century. Ducklings, and sometimes ducks, were served with green peas, either plainly roast and with the peas as an accompaniment, or the two were cooked together in more elaborate dishes. Oranges, olives and peas still make an occasional appearance, but modern palates are exposed to a much wider range of flavours, including those of Asian cultures, in which sweetish, spicy flavours, such as star anise, are combined with duck.

Buying, Storage and Preparation

Even a small turkey weighs 4–5kg (8½–11lb) and will feed 8 people easily; monster birds of 8–10kg (17½–22lb) are quite usual, and likely to leave even a large family with a substantial quantity of leftovers. Make sure you have a large enough roasting tin and – if buying very large birds – that the turkey is not too big for your oven.

Most commercial turkeys are white-feathered, largely because British consumers, over the years, have shown a dislike for the dark pits left on the skin after black feathers have been removed. If this does not bother you, and the idea of a bird with slightly more flavour and slightly less breast meat appeals, try to find a black turkey. Often known as a Norfolk Black, the breed was developed in Europe from the turkeys brought back from Mexico by early Spanish explorers. A well-flavoured alternative is a bronze turkey, a cross between an English domestic turkey and a North American wild turkey; first created in the 18th century, the breed has enjoyed a revival since the 1970s. A good butcher should be able to order a free-range black, bronze or white turkey, or you can buy online direct from the producer.

Remove a turkey from the packaging in which it arrives. Put it on a large dish or in a tin, dry with kitchen paper if it seems wet, and also blot the inside, checking that there are no odds and ends that shouldn't be there. Pick over it for any stray feathers and stubs, cover loosely and store in the bottom of the refrigerator. Remove it and allow it to reach room temperature for 1–2 hours before roasting.

Prepare stuffing in advance if it needs to cool before using. Stuff the crop only (not the body), to avoid the risk of heat not penetrating fully to the centre and the potential for food poisoning. The skin on the neck of the bird will have been left long to make a flap that can be folded over the back and sewn down to keep the stuffing in; you might like to make sure this is neatly trimmed. For birds generally, the cook was sometimes instructed to remove the merrythought (wishbone) beforehand, to make carving easier.

Turkey is perhaps the one bird where this is worth the effort, unless your family tradition is to pull the bone and make a wish across the Christmas table. Under the skin, you will find a line between the flesh of the breast (translucent and slightly pink) and the fat (opaque and creamy), forming the apex of a triangle with the point where the wishbone joins the keel of the breastbone. Cut along these lines with a small sharp knife to free the two long sides of the bone and then work the knife carefully around the top and the points where it meets the wing bones, one at either side. Whether you remove the wishbone or not, add the chosen stuffing, moulding it to give the bird a nice plump breast, and pull the skin back, sewing it down with thin string to prevent the stuffing escaping. Add the weight of the stuffing to that of the bird when you calculate the cooking time.

One company, Gressingham, dominates large-scale goose production, but there are a number of small producers scattered across Britain. A goose from a local butcher may well have been produced locally. Most people who like goose enough to eat it annually try to find a farmer who raises them as a hobby or on a small commercial scale, and then stick with that supplier over the years. Frozen goose is available,

and it is possible to produce a reasonable result with one, but somehow they never seem to crisp up as much as the fresh item, so avoid if possible (should you want a goose for Michaelmas, though, it may be the only option). Large supermarkets stock a limited number of geese around Christmas.

A small goose weighs about 5kg (11lb); a large one about 7kg (15lb). The meat over the breast is a relatively shallow layer, so despite their size, they really don't serve more than 6 people (a big one might stretch to 8 people), with little in the way of leftover meat. On the other hand, the meat is both deeper in flavour and much richer than turkey, so portions can be smaller, and you will have enough goose fat to roast potatoes every Sunday for many months, and bones for good stock.

It is best to remove any wrappings as soon as possible. Geese are now usually deprived of their copious down and the last of their feathers by waxing, and are generally very clean. However, it is always a good idea to pick over them for strays and the odd bit of wax.

Intensive methods used for rearing ducks have attracted adverse media attention in recent decades and free-range ducks are gradually becoming more widely available. Assume, however, unless you have proof positive to the contrary, that any duck on sale is intensively produced. Look online and in local butchers, farmers' markets and farm shops to find free-range duck.

In the kitchen and on the plate, duck shares many characteristics with goose, although it is much smaller. It has only a shallow layer of meat over the breastbone and yields a lot of fat, but has a delicious flavour and a skin that can be roasted to a pleasing crisp texture. Even a relatively large duck will serve only 4 people.

When cooking duck, what everyone wants is crisp skin with moist meat underneath. This is difficult to achieve; more usually, the skin is soggy and the meat perfect, or the skin is cooked to a crisp and the meat is completely dried out. One can remove the skin and crisp it up separately (see page 149).

Roasting and Carving

It is important that turkeys are properly cooked, but the meat has a tendency to dryness, which long cooking exacerbates. Methods suggested for counteracting this include marinating, barding, basting, and slow, gentle cooking. Marinating overnight in flavoured brine can help retain moisture. Bard with streaky bacon, a butter-soaked cloth, or simply smear softened butter over the breast of the bird (especially if you intend to cook it

lying on its back all the time). Basting by pouring the cooking juices and fat back over the bird fairly frequently is a good idea. Also effective is to turn the bird occasionally to complete cooking. Temperatures and times recommended for turkey vary enormously, and depend partly on size. As a guideline, I use 170°C, 325°F, Gas mark 3 for 30 minutes per 500g, but, as ever, be guided by personal experience, the quirks of individual ovens and instinct at the time.

Large turkeys are heavy and difficult to handle when hot. When the bird is fully cooked, leave it to rest, covered, in a warm place. To carve, take slices of breast from back to front. Carve any stuffing in the crop across in slices. Then take off the legs and the wings (with a narrow outer portion of breast attached), and divide like those of a chicken, carving slices off the thighs and drumsticks.

Duck needs a particularly strong heat to start it, so give it 20 minutes at 230°C, 450°F, Gas mark 8 before reducing the heat to 180°C, 350°F, Gas mark 4 and cooking for another 1–1½ hours depending on size; longer cooking helps to produce crisp skin but may dry out the meat. Poultry shears can be used to cut the bird into quarters when cooked. To roast goose, see the recipe on page 129.

The Italian Way of Roasting a Turkey

SERVES 8

4.5kg (10lb) oven-ready turkey

30g (1oz) unsalted butter

2–3 rashers unsmoked bacon

1 large carrot, chopped

1 onion, peeled and chopped

1 small white turnip, chopped

2 celery sticks, chopped

3 garlic cloves, peeled and
      chopped

2 large fresh rosemary sprigs

4–5 cloves

500ml (18fl oz) Giblet Stock
      (see page 119)

salt

1–2 tablespoons arrowroot

FOR THE STUFFING

unsalted butter

about 100g (4oz) unsmoked
      bacon, rind removed,
      chopped in small pieces

about 100g (4oz) good-quality
      sausage meat

100g (4oz) chestnut purée

3 prunes, pitted and chopped

1 small hard pear, peeled
      and chopped

75ml (3fl oz) Marsala

salt and pepper

To make the stuffing, melt the butter, add the bacon and sausage meat, and fry gently for a few minutes. Stir in the chestnut purée, prunes, pear and Marsala, and season with a little salt and plenty of pepper. Cool and then use to stuff the crop.

To cook the turkey, use a stout roasting tin. Smear the butter over the base, and put the bacon and vegetables in. Add the garlic, rosemary and cloves. Put in the turkey on its back, and add stock to cover the base of the tin. Season. Cover the whole with a sheet of foil, crimping it firmly. Put the tin on the hob on the lowest heat. Braise the bird, gently, for about 1½ hours. Check occasionally, adding more liquid if necessary.

Preheat the oven to 180–190°C, 350–375°F, Gas mark 4–5. Move the turkey, still in the covered container, into the oven, and cook for another 45–60 minutes. Remove the foil, baste well, salt the skin and finish roasting, uncovered, for another 45 minutes. Add a little liquid if the juices look dry. When cooked, allow to rest. Tip everything left in the tin through a sieve, catching the juices in a bowl. Press with the back of a wooden spoon to extract any liquid. Put the juices in a pan. Add about 250ml (9fl oz) stock. Finish by slaking the arrowroot with a little cold water; stir this into the gravy and reheat until just boiling and lightly thickened.

Alderman in Chains

This is based on a recipe given by Mrs Roundell in her Practical Cookery Book *(1898),
although the idea of a green herb stuffing goes back much further. These quantities are
about right for a small turkey.*

SERVES 8

1 oven-ready turkey, about
    4.5–5kg (10–11lb)
75g (3oz) unsalted butter,
    softened
8 sausages in a string
splash of stock or hot water,
    to deglaze
1–2 tablespoons arrowroot

FOR THE STUFFING

150g (5oz) stale breadcrumbs
1 dessertspoon finely
    chopped fresh thyme
    or marjoram leaves
1 tablespoon finely
    chopped parsley
grated zest of ½ lemon
    (preferably unwaxed)
75g (3oz) beef suet, or
    unsalted butter broken
    into small pieces
1–2 medium eggs, beaten
1 teaspoon salt
freshly ground black pepper

For the stuffing, mix all ingredients together, adding the eggs
last, to give a soft mixture. Use this to stuff the crop of the
turkey, then sew the skin closed over it.

Preheat the oven to 170°C, 325°F, Gas mark 3. Calculate the
roasting time (see page 123). Spread the softened butter over
the bird and season well. Place it on one side in the roasting tin.
Cook for about 45 minutes, basting every 15 minutes. Turn it
onto the other side and baste well, then cook for another
45 minutes. Turn it onto its back and baste again, then
protect the breast with a piece of foil and continue to
cook, basting regularly.

About 45 minutes before the end of cooking time, put the
sausages into a baking tray (don't cut the links) and put them
in the oven to cook. About 15 minutes before the end of cooking
time, remove the foil from the turkey and allow the skin to
brown. When the bird is fully cooked, rest for 20 minutes.
Check the sausages, keeping them in a string.

Skim off any fat from the cooking juices and add the stock to
the roasting tin. Bring to the boil, scraping the tin. Mix the
arrowroot with a little cold water and add to the juices. Heat
gently until the arrowroot has become translucent and
thickened the gravy.

Present the bird with the string of sausages draped over the
breast or around its front – the 'chains' of the pouting alderman.

French Stuffing

An alternative stuffing for turkey, for those who like a meaty, savoury flavour. It can also be used for veal, or for rabbit or hare. For veal, use more sweet herbs; for rabbit or hare, add 300ml (10fl oz) cream. The original of this delicious recipe was given by John Thacker in 1758. About a century later, Eliza Acton was quoting essentially the same recipe, although without the typically 18th-century addition of anchovies. I've left them in, as it seems to suit modern tastes. Thacker was not specific about the uses of his recipe, but suggested replacing the veal with beef suet for stuffing a turkey – which would render the mixture inedibly fatty to us. Better to stick with veal, or if that is unobtainable, use chicken. Cooked lean veal left over from a roast can be used.

SERVES 6–8

75g (3oz) unsalted butter
2–3 open mushrooms,
  chopped (optional)
the liver of the bird, chopped
  (optional)
150g (5oz) lean cooked veal
  or chicken, minced
1 large teaspoon chopped
  fresh parsley
½ teaspoon fresh thyme leaves
grated zest of ½ lemon
2 anchovies, chopped
a pinch of grated nutmeg
a pinch of cayenne pepper
a pinch of ground mace
50g (2oz) breadcrumbs
a little stock or gravy
30g (1oz) unsmoked bacon,
  chopped
1 medium egg yolk
salt (optional)

Heat 50g (2oz) of the butter in a small frying pan. Cook the mushrooms and liver for a few minutes, then add the veal or chicken, parsley, thyme, lemon zest and anchovies. Season fairly generously with nutmeg and add a pinch of cayenne, a little mace and the breadcrumbs. Allow to cool, then tip into a food processor and whizz to a paste, adding a little stock if the mixture seems dry. Mix in the remaining butter, bacon and the egg yolk.

Note that Thacker says, 'take care you don't season it too high'. The best way to find out if the seasoning is right is to fry a trial spoonful and taste it. Only then add salt if you consider it necessary, as the anchovies and bacon will have contributed some saltiness already.

Chestnut Stuffing

Chestnut stuffings go back at least as far as the first half of the 19th century in English cookery. This one is based on a recipe given by Eliza Acton (in 1845) and is good for turkey and game.

SERVES 8

150g (5oz) chestnut purée
75g (3oz) unsmoked bacon,
  chopped
50g (2oz) stale white
  breadcrumbs
grated zest of ½ lemon
  (preferably unwaxed)

a pinch of freshly grated
  nutmeg
a pinch of cayenne pepper
1 medium egg
1 teaspoon salt
a little stock or milk

Mix together all the ingredients except the stock to make a smooth paste. If it seems a little on the dry side, stir in some stock or milk to slacken the mixture a little. It can be used as stuffing or made into 8 little cakes, floured and then fried gently.

Almond Sauce

Another excellent recipe from The Gentle Art of Cookery *by Mrs Leyel and Miss Hartley (1925), whose book also provided* The Italian Way of Roasting a Turkey *(see page 124). Nut sauces for all sorts of meat recur in Middle Eastern and Indian cookery.*

SERVES 6

30g (1oz) unsalted butter
100g (4oz) ground almonds
30g (1oz) plain flour
250–300ml (9–10fl oz) stock
a pinch of ground mace
a little salt
2 tablespoons single cream
  (optional)

Melt the butter in a heavy saucepan over low heat and stir in the almonds. Cook very gently, stirring all the time, until the almonds are browned and toasted. Stir in the flour, then add the stock and continue to cook and stir until the mixture comes to the boil. Season with a little mace (which really does enhance this recipe) and salt. Finish by adding cream if you have some available.

Roast Goose

Geese are large birds and the amount of fat they yield during cooking is startling. Make sure the oven is big enough. You will need a deep roasting tin, a rack, a pair of sturdy oven gloves and a capacious bowl for the fat. A supply of heavy-duty foil is also useful. Allow 30 minutes per 500g.

SERVES 6

1 goose
salt and pepper
stuffing, as required
Giblet Stock (see page 119)
2 tablespoons arrowroot

About 1 hour before you want to start cooking the bird, allow it to come to room temperature. Preheat the oven to 220°C, 425°F, Gas mark 7. Rub the bird with salt and pepper and stuff the body. Place the goose on a rack in a deep roasting tin. Start it breast downwards. Use foil to extend the tin under any of the goose that projects over the edge (it's also useful for wrapping round wing tips and ends of drumsticks if they show signs of browning too fast).

Put the goose into the oven and cook for 30 minutes, then turn the heat down to 180–190°C, 350–375°F, Gas mark 4–5 and continue to roast. After 30 minutes, remove from the oven and ladle the fat out of the roasting tin into a bowl. Turn the goose onto its back. Return it to the oven and continue to cook. Keep checking the fat in the roasting tin, and pour it off into a bowl from time to time. When cooked, rest for about 20 minutes.

To finish the gravy, pour off the fat, returning any browned cooking juices and sediment to the tin. Pour in the stock, stir to deglaze, and bring to the boil. Slake the arrowroot with a little cold water and pour into the gravy. Bring it back to boiling point to thicken. Check the seasoning, then strain into a gravy boat.

Potato and Apple Stuffing

Mashed potatoes are excellent for stuffing goose. French chef Alexis Soyer advocated them in the mid-19th century, in combination with apples, although the idea didn't really become popular in English cookery until the middle of the 20th century.

SERVES 6

75g (3oz) unsalted butter

1 large onion, peeled
   and chopped

600g (1¼lb) floury potatoes,
   peeled and
   cut into chunks

2 garlic cloves, peeled
   and crushed

1 tablespoon chopped
   fresh sage

1 teaspoon salt

freshly ground black pepper

2 large apples (Cox's or a
   dryish, aromatic eating
   apple), peeled, cored and
   cut into chunks

Melt the butter in a large frying pan, then add the onion and cook gently until it begins to brown.

Boil the potatoes and mash. Stir in the cooked onion, the crushed garlic, sage, salt and a generous seasoning of pepper. Mix the pieces of apple through the mixture, and use to stuff the goose.

Chestnut and Prune Stuffing

Chestnut stuffing is more commonly associated with turkey, but can also be very good with goose. The same is true for prunes, which are quite often used with goose in continental Europe. Like potato stuffing, this didn't make much of an impact in British cookery until the mid-20th century.

SERVES 6–8

15g (½oz) unsalted butter
1–2 shallots, peeled and
    finely chopped
1 garlic clove, peeled
    and crushed
200–250g (7–9oz) chestnut
    purée (tinned is fine)
200–250g (7–9oz) sausage meat
1 scant teaspoon salt
freshly ground black pepper
12 prunes (ready-to-eat, or
    soaked dried ones), pitted
2 large apples (Cox's or a
    dryish, aromatic eating
    apple), peeled, cored and
    cut in thick slices

Melt the butter in a small pan and fry the shallots and garlic lightly. Put the chestnut purée in a bowl and break it up. Mix in the shallots and garlic, sausage meat, salt and a generous seasoning of pepper.

Put half this mixture into the goose, then add the prunes and apples in a layer, and spread the remainder of the stuffing over them.

Orange Sauce for Roast Duck

Over the centuries, many cultures have devised ways for cooking and serving duck with fruity and sweet–acid flavours. Seville oranges are best, with both tame and wild duck. Their season is very limited – they come onto the market in mid-December and vanish by the end of January – but they can be frozen. This orange sauce is based on one given by Martha Bradley in 1756.

SERVES 4

100ml (3½fl oz) port
the cooking juices from the
    bird, skimmed of fat
juice of 2 Seville oranges
juice of 1 lemon
salt and pepper

Deglaze the roasting tin with the port and pour all into a small pan. Add the juices from cooking the bird and the orange and lemon juice, and bring to the boil. Taste, and season with salt and pepper. Serve with the duck and a sweetish vegetable accompaniment, such as roast parsnips, or perhaps boiled potatoes and boiled parsnips mashed together.

Slow-Roast Duck Legs with Marmalade

The orange flavourings can also be used to marinate portions of duck.

SERVES 4

4 duck legs
1 generous tablespoon bitter
    orange marmalade
juice of 1 (sweet) orange
juice of 1 lemon
a little stock (optional)
salt and pepper

Put the duck legs in an ovenproof dish that holds them neatly. Mix the marmalade, orange and lemon juices, and pour over the duck. Cover and leave in the refrigerator to marinate for 24 hours. Stir from time to time to make sure the duck is well coated with marinade.

Cook the duck legs at 140°C, 275°F, Gas mark 1 for 1¾ hours, turning them after 1 hour. About 15 minutes before the end of cooking time, pour the fat and cooking juices into a bowl and turn up the heat to 170°C, 325°F, Gas mark 3 to crisp the skin.

When the duck legs are ready, remove them to a serving plate. Skim the fat off the reserved cooking juices and use the latter to deglaze the roasting dish (you may want to add a little stock or water to help the process along, but don't overdo it – there should be a relatively small quantity of thin, concentrated gravy). Taste, adjust the seasoning, and serve.

TURKEY, GOOSE & DUCK

John Thacker's Sauce for Roast Duck

John Thacker was cook to the Dean and Chapter of Durham Cathedral, who must have eaten rather well to judge from his recipes. A typically savoury, meaty, early 18th-century sauce for those who don't like sweet–sour combinations.

SERVES 4

15g (½oz) unsalted butter

1 medium onion, peeled, halved and thinly sliced

scant 1 dessertspoon plain flour

100ml (3½fl oz) red wine

150ml (5fl oz) well-flavoured duck or chicken stock

1 tablespoon salted capers, rinsed

cooking juices from the duck

Melt the butter in a small frying pan. Add the onion and cook fairly quickly, stirring frequently, until it begins to catch and brown slightly. Sprinkle in the flour and stir well. Stir in the red wine, followed by the stock, and keep stirring until the mixture returns to the boil. Add the capers, then turn the heat down and allow to cook gently for at least 20 minutes. Add a little more stock or water if the mixture evaporates too much; it should be fairly thin.

Any juices from roasting the duck, skimmed of fat, can be added to this sauce just before serving.

LEFTOVERS

Christmas lunch is possibly the one time of the year when the average British household finds itself with vast amounts of leftovers sitting in the refrigerator and demanding ingenuity in the using up, before everyone gets completely bored with the taste of turkey in curries, fricassees, pies, sandwiches and soups. For sandwiches, see also Chicken Sandwiches with Ravigote Butter, page 112.

There are seldom any leftovers from roast duck or goose, which may account for the fact that there are very few recipes for using them in the British cookery repertoire. However, duck, like goose, can yield an astonishing quantity of fat. Pour this off and store in a jar in the refrigerator. Use it for roasting or sautéing potatoes.

TURKEY SOUP

Turkey bones make excellent stock. The slower it is cooked, the better – put the stockpot in a very low oven after the contents have come to the boil, or use a slow cooker, in which case you should get a lovely clear golden broth. It can be used to make this 21st-century version of Eliza Acton's 'Economical turkey soup'. Hers was beefed up (literally) with some fresh beef when making the stock, and served with a little boiled rice in the broth. We'd consider the beef an extravagance, but the suggestion she made about adding ham and 'catsup' (a catch-all name for various condiment sauces imported directly from the Far East) suggested south-east Asian flavours.

SERVES 4

1 litre (1¾ pints) well-flavoured turkey stock
a few celery leaves, finely chopped
about 100g (4oz) ham, diced
1 fresh red chilli pepper, finely diced
2 teaspoons nam pla (Thai fish sauce)
100g (4oz) cooked rice
salt
chopped fresh coriander
lime zest, cut in fine slivers (optional)

Put the turkey stock in a large pan and bring to the boil. Add the celery leaves, ham, chilli pepper and nam pla, and cook for a few minutes. Add the cooked rice just before serving and let it heat through (it can be added earlier, but it makes the stock lose some of its clarity). Taste and add salt if necessary. Ladle into bowls and add a sprinkle of chopped coriander and a little lime zest to each serving.

DEVILLED TURKEY

Particularly good with the brown meat of turkey, devilling was a popular way of dealing with all sorts of meat from the late 18th to the mid-20th century. This recipe is based on one in Mrs A. B. Marshall's Cookery Book, *a classic of the late 19th century.*

SERVES 2

about 250g (9oz) cooked turkey

2 teaspoons Dijon mustard

½ teaspoon English mustard

½ teaspoon salt

2 heaped dessertspoons mango chutney –
　any large pieces of fruit in the chutney
　chopped fine

cayenne pepper, to taste

freshly ground black pepper

Pull the turkey into long, narrow pieces. Mix the mustards, salt, chutney, cayenne and a generous grind of black pepper. Rub the paste into the turkey pieces and leave in a cool place for 1–2 hours.

To cook, put the pieces under a preheated moderate grill for a few minutes. Turn a couple of times, until they are well heated through. Alternatively, put them in a single layer in an ovenproof dish and bake in a hot oven, 220°C, 425°F, Gas mark 7, for 7–10 minutes.

Serve hot with rice and more chutney, or scatter over a salad of mixed leaves.

WHITE DEVIL

SERVES 4

280ml (9½fl oz) single cream

2 tablespoons Worcestershire sauce

1 teaspoon English mustard, or to taste

250g (9oz) cooked turkey breast meat, chopped

fresh green or red chillies (optional)

salt

Put the cream in a saucepan and mix in the Worcestershire sauce and mustard. Heat rapidly until it boils. Stir in the turkey meat and allow to cook, very gently, until it is thoroughly hot. If using fresh chilli, remove the strings and seeds and cut the flesh into fine slivers. Add to the pan, then taste and correct the seasoning. Serve with boiled rice and a salad.

TURKEY PIE

Turkey, chicken or veal and ham combinations are all traditional in pies in English cookery. Add mushrooms, or make a particularly good (if expensive) version by adding some of the white truffle and porcini paste sold in jars in Italian delicatessens.

SERVES 4–6

40g (1½oz) unsalted butter

150g (5oz) button mushrooms, sliced

40g (1½oz) plain flour

350ml (12fl oz) well-flavoured turkey stock

shortcrust pastry made with 100g (4oz)
    unsalted butter and lard mixed, and
    200g (7oz) plain flour

40g (1½oz) white truffle and porcini paste
    (optional)

200–250g (7–9oz) cooked turkey,
    cut in neat pieces

125g (4½oz) cooked ham or gammon,
    cut in dice

1 medium egg, beaten

salt and pepper

Melt the butter in a saucepan and cook the mushrooms until all the liquid they exude has evaporated, but don't allow them to brown. Stir in the flour to make a roux, then add the stock gradually, stirring to produce a sauce. Season to taste and allow to cool.

When ready to bake, preheat the oven to 200°C, 400°F, Gas mark 6, and put a metal baking sheet in to heat. Roll two-thirds of the pastry fairly thin and use it to line a pie dish about 20cm (8in) in diameter.

If using the truffle paste, mix it with the turkey meat. Distribute this, and the ham, over the pastry. Spoon the sauce in on top. Roll out the remaining pastry and use to cover the pie, sealing and crimping the edges. Cut a hole in the top for the steam to escape and decorate the surface of the pie with leaves made from the pastry trimmings. Brush with beaten egg.

Put the pie on the preheated baking sheet and cook for 15–20 minutes to set and crisp the pastry. Then reduce the heat to 180°C, 350°F, Gas mark 4, and bake for 20–25 minutes more. Serve hot or cold.

SALSA FOR TURKEY

Sometimes a 'sauce piquant' was served with devilled food in the 19th century. Recipes for it are based on a reduction of shallots and vinegar in butter, made into a flour-thickened sauce, which was further livened up with pepper, chilli or chopped gherkins. To us, the flavour is a bit contrived, but the vinegar-onion reduction suggested a tomato salsa – which usually contains raw onions, not to everyone's taste.

SERVES 2–4

1 small shallot, peeled and very finely chopped
4 tablespoons white wine vinegar
1–2 tablespoons olive oil
1 beef tomato, skin and seeds removed,
    finely diced
1 garlic clove, peeled and crushed
a little chopped fresh red chilli
a pinch of granulated sugar
salt

Put the shallot and vinegar in a small pan and boil rapidly until the vinegar has evaporated. Pour into a small bowl and stir in the oil and tomato. Add the garlic and the chilli to taste, plus a pinch of sugar and a little salt.

This can be served with Devilled Turkey (see page 138), or added to a Club Sandwich (see below).

CLUB SANDWICH

Use three slices of toast per sandwich; spread the bottom layer with a little mayonnaise, add salad leaves (flat lettuce or lamb's lettuce), and 2–3 rashers crisp bacon; add a second layer of toast, then spread with a little more mayonnaise, top with thinly sliced turkey breast and a layer of salsa, and top with a final layer of toast. Press down firmly and cut obliquely to make triangular sandwiches.

CURRY

There are so many curry pastes and marinades available that it may seem a bit redundant to give a recipe, but here is a delicious one based on Colonel Kenney-Herbert's spicing for a mild, coconut-flavoured Ceylon curry (he suggested it for fish, shellfish, chicken or 'any nice white meat'). A former army officer in India, he devoted a chapter of his book, Common-Sense Cookery (1905) *to curries. It can be spiced up with more chilli if desired.*

SERVES 4

250–300g (9–10oz) onions, peeled and
    very finely chopped
50g (2oz) unsalted butter
1 teaspoon ground turmeric
2 teaspoons ground coriander
1 teaspoon ground cinnamon
½ teaspoon ground cardamom seeds
½ teaspoon chilli powder
½ teaspoon freshly ground black pepper
½ teaspoon salt
1 tablespoon grated fresh root ginger
400ml (14fl oz) coconut milk
400g (14oz) cooked turkey, cut in
    bite-sized chunks

Put the onions and butter in a heatproof casserole and fry gently until the onions begin to turn gold. Add the spices and salt, and cook gently for about 5 minutes, then add the ginger. Stir in the coconut milk and bring to the boil to make a smooth sauce. Allow this to cook gently for a few minutes longer, then stir in the turkey and continue to simmer for about 15 minutes so that the sauce reduces a little. It shouldn't be too runny.

Serve with rice and salad.

PICKLED PEARS

MAKES 400G

400g (14oz) hard pears (under-ripe
    Conference, or similar)
100g (4oz) light soft brown sugar
grated zest of ½ lemon (preferably unwaxed)
100ml (3½fl oz) white wine vinegar
    or cider vinegar
4 cloves, bruised
10 black peppercorns, bruised

Peel, core and cut the pears into chunks. Place all the ingredients in a pan and bring to the boil. Boil, uncovered, for 20–30 minutes, or until the pieces of pear are soft. Mash them into the liquid a little to help them break down. The result should have a slightly jammy consistency.

Eat immediately, or keep in the refrigerator for up to 2 weeks. Serve with cold roast goose.

ALEXIS SOYER'S HASHED GOOSE

There are few recipes for using up the meat from a cold roast goose in the British repertoire – perhaps because the bird doesn't feed that many people at one sitting. Even the great 19th-century chef Alexis Soyer flagged somewhat when contemplating leftover goose, suggesting this simple recipe.

SERVES 2

15g (½oz) unsalted butter or goose fat
½ small onion, peeled and finely chopped
1 dessertspoon plain flour
250ml (9fl oz) well-flavoured stock,
    preferably goose (see page 119)
about 250g (9oz) leftover cooked goose,
    cut in slices
2–3 fresh sage leaves, torn into pieces
salt and pepper

Melt the butter in a large saucepan and fry the onion gently until soft. Stir in the flour and cook for a few minutes, then add the stock and stir to make a sauce. Add the cooked goose and the sage. Simmer gently until all is hot, then taste and adjust the seasoning. Serve with mashed potato.

GOOSE SALAD

Don't put any large pieces of goose skin in the stockpot. Remove it from the bird and cut into neat pieces about 1cm (½in) wide and 2cm (¾in) long. Put these in a baking tray with a lip (they will yield quite a lot of fat), sprinkle with salt, and cook in a hot oven at 220°C, 425°F, Gas mark 7. Look at them after 7–10 minutes, when they should have crisped up. Thicker pieces may need a little longer. Drain on kitchen paper and scatter over mashed potatoes, or use in a salad, such as this one, with any bits of leftover cooked goose.

SERVES 2

1 large eating apple, such as Cox's or a russet
½ celery stick
1 teaspoon very finely chopped onion or shallot
12 walnut halves, broken up a little
cold roast goose, shredded
skin from a roast goose, cooked until crisp

FOR THE DRESSING
1 teaspoon smooth Dijon mustard
a pinch of salt
a little lemon zest (preferably unwaxed),
    finely grated
1 dessertspoon white wine vinegar or
    cider vinegar
4 dessertspoons walnut or olive oil

Peel and core the apple, and cut into chunks of about 1cm (½in). Cut the celery into similarly sized pieces. Mix with the onion and the walnut pieces. Add the leftover goose.

Blend the mustard, salt, lemon zest, vinegar and oil to make a dressing, and toss with the apple mixture. Scatter the crisp goose skin on top.

ONION SOUP

The broth from goose is good for a vegetable or lentil soup, or in recipes normally requiring a beef stock. It is better to reduce it by slow simmering to about two-thirds of the original amount. This soup is based on a recipe from The Experienced English Housewife *(1769) by Mrs Raffald, once a housekeeper at Arley Hall in Cheshire and later a professional confectioner and outside caterer in Manchester. A cousin, perhaps, of French onion soup, it responds well to the toast-and-cheese treatment when serving. The recipe also works well with beef or duck stock.*

SERVES 2

2 large Spanish onions – total weight
    about 1kg (2¼lb)
50g (2oz) unsalted butter
1 litre (1¾ pints) well-flavoured goose stock
salt and pepper
2 medium egg yolks
2 tablespoons cider vinegar

FOR SERVING
bread for toast (slices from an ordinary loaf
    is fine, but use ciabatta or French bread
    if you prefer)
Cheddar cheese, grated

Peel the onions, removing all the papery outer skin plus the layer immediately underneath (which has a tendency to dry out and become hard during cooking). Slice them thinly. Melt the butter in a large pan and add the onions, stir well and cover. Cook on the lowest possible heat for 45–60 minutes, stirring from time to time. The onions should not colour, but become very soft.

Add the stock, bring to the boil, and simmer gently for about 15 minutes. Taste and season. Draw the pan off the heat.

Beat the egg yolks with the vinegar and add to the soup, stirring thoroughly. Once the yolks have been added, the soup should not be allowed to boil again, but should be reheated cautiously until very hot and slightly thickened (don't overdo it, or the egg will curdle).

Just before serving, toast the bread, cover it with grated Cheddar and toast gently until the cheese has melted. Cut into neat pieces and float some on top of each bowl of soup.

DUCK AND GREEN PEA SALAD

Should the duck skin have refused to crisp up properly, or if there is a fairly large amount of leftover skin, try roasting it in the oven as with the goose skin for the Goose Salad (see page 146). Drain on kitchen paper and scatter over a watercress salad, or mashed potatoes, or try this modern take on the idea of duck with green peas. It can be used to make a small salad for just one person, using the pickings off a duck carcass, or scaled up if more meat is available.

SERVES 1

50g (2oz) cold duck, picked free of skin
    and fat, cut in slivers
crisp duck skin
a piece of cucumber about 4cm (1½in) long,
    cut in batons
50g (2oz) cooked peas
1 spring onion, trimmed and cut
    obliquely in thin slices
1cm (½in) cube fresh root ginger, peeled
    and cut in thin slivers
a piece of red chilli pepper (to taste),
    cut in tiny dice or slivers
chopped fresh coriander, to garnish

FOR THE DRESSING
½ teaspoon nam pla (Thai fish sauce)
1 teaspoon rice vinegar
2 teaspoons neutral-flavoured oil,
    such as sunflower
a pinch of granulated sugar

Mix the dressing ingredients together, then toss with the duck, duck skin, cucumber, peas, spring onion, ginger and chilli, and scatter with coriander.

BEETROOT SOUP

Beetroot soup is not a British tradition; it arrived, usually as a variation on Eastern European borscht, in the early 20th century, as part of an 'international' cookery repertoire. This version is based, very loosely, on one given by Sir Harry Luke in The Tenth Muse *(first published in 1954). The soup is better if the stock is clarified, but it is not absolutely essential. The stock does need to be well flavoured, though, so if you can acquire some extra giblets or bones when making it, it will give a better soup. Use duck, goose or beef stock.*

SERVES 3–4

1 large raw beetroot, trimmed and peeled

1 medium carrot, trimmed and peeled

½ small red onion, peeled

2 garlic cloves, peeled

a thumb-sized piece of fresh root ginger, peeled

1 litre (1¾ pints) well-flavoured stock,
    preferably clarified

2 tablespoons soy sauce

1 tablespoon red wine vinegar

½ teaspoon muscovado sugar

zest of ½ orange (preferably unwaxed),
    cut into very thin strips

salt

sour cream, to serve

Cut the beetroot and carrot into julienne (long matchstick) strips. Slice the onion very thinly, cut the garlic into fine slivers, and cut the ginger into very thin strips.

Put the stock in a pan and heat, adding all the prepared vegetables. Bring to a simmer and allow to cook for a few minutes. Add the soy sauce, wine vinegar, sugar and orange zest. Taste and check for seasoning: add more of the flavourings if desired, or a little salt if you think the soy sauce hasn't given enough.

Serve with a spoonful of sour cream in each bowl.

Game

Game is our collective term for wild animals and birds that are hunted. It encompasses a wide range – from very small birds suitable for one portion, such as snipe, up to large beasts such as red deer. Game birds in Britain are pheasant, partridge, grouse, pigeon, woodcock, snipe and several species of wild duck. Game animals include rabbit and hare, and the meat of several deer species – most importantly red, fallow and roe deer. Wild boar have also been reintroduced to Britain as farmed animals.

Since the Middle Ages, there has always been some management of game species. Methods over the years have included controlling predators and encouraging specific environments, such as grouse moors and parks for deer. Some animals that were originally farmed, such as rabbits, have now made their home in the wild; ones that were once exclusively wild beasts, such as red deer, are now farmed; others, such as pheasants, are reared and fed in such large numbers for shoots that they are semi-domesticated.

Game Birds

The good flavour of game birds was prized for stock-making in kitchens of the past. In the 18th century, partridges were often added to the general brew of meats for the rich gravies and meat coulis that seem to have flavoured or accompanied almost every meat at the table. In the 19th century, older birds, unsuitable for roasting, were often used as a basis for consommé. Methods for roasting, though, always seem to have been plain and unadorned.

Game provides flavours and textures outside the variety of domestic birds, and meat that is very definitely free-range.

Rabbit and Hare

Rabbits are not native to the British Isles, something that may seem surprising when one considers how they breed in our countryside – like, well, rabbits. Formerly they were considered a delicacy, carefully nurtured in warrens; then they escaped and became pests. In the 19th century, they were the only wild meat available to the rural poor, although even taking rabbits was sometimes regarded as poaching. Hares are native, and they and the rabbit population occupy roughly the same ecological niche, although the two species seem to have a slightly uneasy balance as to which dominates in the countryside.

Rabbit and hare meat was noted for its leanness and dryness, and in the past was usually larded. The heads were left on (but skinned) for roasting. A hare was usually stuffed, with the head set upright and the ears propped so they stood erect, a custom that must have provided endless trouble for the person tending the spit. Illustrations from 18th- and 19th-century cookery books show how they should be served, looking a little astonished by the whole thing. Both hares and rabbits sometimes had their body cavities lined with streaky bacon before cooking. The juices from roast hare tend to curdle during cooking, and an initial basting of milk or cream was often recommended 'to draw away the blood', the sauce being made with butter, claret and gravy from some other animal.

Venison

'Venison' once meant the flesh of any wild mammal hunted for food, and so technically would have included hare and animals such as wild boar. It has now come to apply specifically to the meat of deer. The right to hunt these animals was a jealously guarded privilege of the aristocracy in the past, and few ordinary people tasted the meat, unless poached.

Venison was a mark of status, and there were many attempts to imitate it by marinating beef and mutton. The meat tends to dryness, and the real thing was often larded, wrapped in paper and then enclosed in a 'huff' paste – a coarse pastry made of plain flour and water, sometimes with a little beef suet – before putting

it to roast in front of an open fire. A sweet-sour sauce of venison gravy, port wine and a little sugar, was served with it in the 18th century. Keeping venison well was a great preoccupation, and early cookery books include instructions for how to prevent it tainting, usually by rubbing with black pepper and ginger.

The 19th-century fashion for things Scottish led to the development of deer-stalking as a 'sport', and also saw the introduction of smaller species of deer, including sika and muntjac, mostly as ornamental animals in the parkland of country estates. Two factors have made venison more accessible since the 1980s. One is the development of deer farming, from small beginnings in the 1960s. The other is an increase in population among various deer species, especially red deer in the Scottish Highlands and roe deer in southern England.

Buying Game Birds

Pheasants can be extremely cheap (especially if you live near a large shoot and can dress them yourself). This is because pheasant chicks are often hatched indoors and given extra feed after they are released into the woods, which has vastly increased their availability and decreased their price. Grouse, woodcock and snipe, however, remain very expensive.

All birds intended for roasting should be young ones. You will have to trust the game dealer, and buy earlier in the season rather than later. Game from the wild (except pigeon and rabbit) is also subject to laws restricting the times of year when it can be shot. Outside the following seasons, frozen game is often available; look online for specialist retailers:

- grouse: 12 August–10 December
- snipe: 12 August–31 January
- mallard, teal, widgeon:
  1 September–31 January
- partridge: 1 September–1 February
- woodcock: 1 October–31 January
- pheasant: 1 October–1 February

Hanging game both develops the flavour and helps to tenderise the flesh. Birds are hung by the neck, complete with feathers and insides, in a cool, airy place. Hanging time depends on the weather (a longer time is required in cold weather), the species and age of the bird and is also, to some extent, a matter of taste. The old method of telling if a pheasant was sufficiently well hung was to try pulling one of the tail feathers: if it came out easily, the bird was judged to be at the correct stage. Some households took things to extremes, and people who had worked as kitchen staff in the late 19th and early 20th centuries would tell of pheasants hung until they were very 'high' indeed. Not nice for those who had to dress them, however ambrosial the flavour may have been considered. It is unlikely that a purchased pheasant would now be hung for more than 7–10 days, except by special request. Partridge and grouse need only 2–3 days.

Buying game is something of a lottery. If some game birds are now relatively inexpensive, this is partly because they are prepared quickly, in large numbers and with the aid of machines. This is understandable: plucking and eviscerating are not pleasant jobs, but if they are done carefully and neatly, the birds look nicer, and the skin will crisp better.

A pheasant will serve 4 people. Allow one grey-legged partridge per person; a red-legged one may be larger, but it is still probably safer to allow one per person. Though relatively large and meaty, allow one grouse per person. Wild duck varies in size according to species, but most of the meat is on the breast (in common with most waterfowl) and is on the shallow side. Allow one bird for 2 people.

Roasting Game Birds

The old expression relating to the cooking of small game birds and wild duck was that they 'should just fly through the kitchen'. Cookery books usually state that game birds, especially small ones such as partridge and grouse, should be served rare (with the breast meat pink or just done). This is not to everyone's taste, and can leave the legs quite underdone. If you wish to serve the birds whole, then you may have to compromise: if you would like the legs to be cooked through, the breast meat will be more cooked with some risk of dryness; if you would like the breast meat to be just done, the legs may be very underdone. Resting the bird helps. Alternatively – although purists would frown on this – carve off the breasts from the birds after a short rest, return the birds to the oven for a few minutes, then carve the legs and serve piled up on a crouton.

When serving grouse, remember that their flavour is rich, and almost all cookery books advise that they should be served very rare, but the leg meat of grouse can be bitter when undercooked, and the heathery flavour overpowering. Both these characteristics diminish as the bird approaches the medium stage of done-ness. Unless you are certain that you like the taste, it can be better to cook until the leg meat is fully done.

For roasting, season the bird, inside and out, with salt and pepper. Add a squeeze of lemon juice to the body cavity (or a sprig of thyme for grouse). Bard with bacon or spread butter over the breast. Put the birds on their backs in a roasting tin just large enough to hold them; do not cover. Roast according to the times and temperatures given below.

About 10 minutes before the end of cooking, remove any bacon from the breast of the birds, baste well and dust with flour to froth them (see page 17). When cooked to your liking (check the colour of the flesh between the thigh and body of the bird to ascertain how well done they are), remove the birds to a hot serving dish and keep warm.

Tip off as much fat as possible from the roasting tin. If the flour from frothing the birds hasn't fallen into the tin, add about 1 teaspoon to the residues and stir it in over gentle heat to cook and brown slightly. Then stir in 250ml (9fl oz) well-flavoured chicken stock. Bring to the boil and cook gently for a few minutes. Check the seasoning. The gravy should be clear, thin and well flavoured.

Serve grouse on toast, one piece per bird. Should you have the livers of the grouse, cook lightly in butter, then season and mash and spread over the toast before serving.

Roasting Times
and Temperatures

- Pheasants: start at 200°C, 400°F,
  Gas mark 6 for 20 minutes, then
  reduce to 180°C, 350°F, Gas mark 4
  for 20–30 minutes. Don't overcook,
  as they become dry, tough and
  flavourless.
- Partridges: start at 200°C, 400°F,
  Gas mark 6 for 10 minutes, then
  reduce to 180°C, 350°F, Gas mark 4 for
  10–15 minutes, or until done to taste.
  Partridges have a rich and distinctive
  flavour. There are two species available:
  the native grey-legged, and the slightly
  larger French red-legged partridge,
  a bird introduced to south-eastern
  England. Both make good eating, but
  they must be young for roasting, and
  the red-legged needs care to make sure
  it doesn't dry out.
- Grouse: start at 200°C, 400°F,
  Gas mark 6 for 10–15 minutes, then
  reduce to 180°C, 350°F, Gas mark 4
  for 10–15 minutes.
- Wild ducks (teal, widgeon): start
  at 200°C, 400°F, Gas mark 6 for
  10 minutes, then reduce to 180°C,
  350°F, Gas mark 4 for 10–15 minutes.
- Mallard: start at 200°C, 400°F, Gas
  mark 6 for 15 minutes, then reduce
  to 180°C, 350°F, Gas mark 4 for about
  25 minutes.

Buying and Roasting
Rabbit and Hare

Most rabbits sold in Britain are wild
ones and their roasting qualities are
uncertain. Active lives can be reflected
in lean, dry meat and an excessively
rabbity flavour. Treat them gently:
marinades are useful for counteracting
dryness and adding flavour; stuffing or
barding also adds fat and flavour. They
need to be roasted at a low temperature
for about 1–1½ hours.

Wild rabbits weigh from 500g (1lb
2oz) to 1kg (2¼lb); the heavier ones will
be about right for 4 people. Most of the
meat is in the hind legs and the saddle,
as the forequarter contains too much
bone to be rewarding. The creature will
usually arrive skinned and paunched
but should still contain the 'pluck' – the
kidneys, liver, lungs and heart. Discard
the lungs. The liver and kidneys are
delicacies, and can be incorporated
into a stuffing mixture or used to make
stock or sauce. Note that farmed rabbits
are usually imported, some from very
intensive systems.

Hares should not be confused with
rabbits, least of all in the kitchen. Hares
are bigger, with dark meaty flesh and a
rich, strong flavour. They are seasonal,
and are available fresh from August
to February.

A hare should hang for about 1 week. Only young ones (leverets) are tender enough for roasting, so you need to be able to trust your game dealer or butcher about this. A hare will also be sold with the pluck in place, and sometimes be accompanied by a little container with the blood of the animal (used for thickening moist-cooked dishes such as jugged hare, but not in roasting). Remove the pluck; use the liver in stuffing, and the rest in stock. Hare should be well cooked, and if roasted whole, the forelegs should be drawn back and the hind legs forwards and held in place with skewers through the body (the sinews under the legs need to be cut to achieve this).

A whole hare will weigh 2–2.5kg (4½–5lb), and feed 6 people easily. See page 175 for roasting time and temperature. They are sometimes divided into forequarters and a joint comprising the saddle and hindquarters: count the ribs forwards from the back, and cut after the sixth rib (use the forequarters for a different slow-cooked dish, such as soup or jugged hare). For a small, neat joint of the saddle only, remove the hind legs with slanting cuts across them, from the tail to where the thigh joins the side of the body. A heavy cleaver will be needed to cut through the backbone, so you may prefer a butcher to joint the animal.

Hare responds well to marinating, and can be left for 2–3 days in a marinade, either in a cold place or in the refrigerator. It is still a good idea to lard it, and using lardons rolled in a seasoning mixture takes both fat and flavour deep into the meat. Should you lack the wherewithal or time to lard, then bard with a few pieces of bacon instead. Use very thinly sliced, very streaky bacon for barding (cut using an old-fashioned bacon slicer). If you can't obtain this, it is better to use pancetta than a chunkily sliced ordinary bacon. Whichever you choose, it should be unsmoked.

Redcurrant jelly or other fruit jellies, such as quince or rowanberry, make excellent accompaniments for hare.

The best meat in both hares and rabbits is in the saddle, lying on either side of and parallel to the backbone. Carve this in long, thin slices. Smaller slices can be cut from the hind legs. The shoulders should be taken off by dividing the joint from the ribs.

Buying and Roasting Venison

Farmed red deer venison is the most easily available, sold through supermarkets, butchers and online, but wild red deer venison also reaches the market and can be found online from specialist online retailers, who may also be able to provide roe, fallow and smaller species such as sika and muntjac.

Deer farming does not involve complete domestication of the animals, and they feed principally on grass. In terms of welfare, the meat is raised to high standards. Red deer venison should be hung for 2 weeks, as venison bought from a deer farm almost certainly will have been. Wild red deer venison will be leaner and less predictable in quality, but provided it has been carefully stalked and hung, it should be excellent. If you have the choice, buck venison is considered finer than doe. Venison generally is a dark-red, fine-grained meat, which is very lean and low in saturated fat.

Cuts for roasting vary greatly in size according to species. Those from red deer are largest; a saddle from this animal will be too large for many domestic ovens and is usually split down the backbone and divided into loin and best end. Saddles from smaller species are left whole. The haunch (hind leg) is also a prime cut. These joints are best slightly underdone. Shoulder makes a good slow roast.

Venison has the potential to be extremely dry when roasted: larding repays the effort required. Marinating, often recommended for venison, may have become popular because it acted as a short-term preservation method in the past.

Carving venison from the smaller species is similar to carving mutton or lamb, although saddle or loin of red deer should be carved like sirloin of beef. Venison is best served on very hot plates so it doesn't cool, ideally with French beans which complements the flavour of the meat. Redcurrant jelly is a traditional accompaniment for roast venison, but other fruit jellies, such as gooseberry or sloe, go well too.

Making Stock from Game Bones

If all you have available is the leftovers from roasting a few partridge or a brace of grouse, it is still possible to make stock. Collect all the bones, skin and debris of the birds and put in a suitable pan. The remains of 4 partridge or 2 grouse will produce about 750ml (1¼ pints) of well-flavoured stock. 3–4 tablespoons of sherry, port or wine will improve the stock – add it and heat until it boils, then add 1 litre (1¾ pints) of water. Also add a piece of onion; a few black peppercorns; a bouquet garni made of bay leaf, parsley stalks and thyme sprigs; a small carrot; and some ham trimmings if you have them. Simmer very gently for 1½–2 hours, topping up with fresh water if necessary, or use a slow cooker. Strain the stock, measure it and (if necessary) reduce by fast boiling. Venison or hare bones can be used in the same way.

Roast Woodcock or Snipe

Woodcock is thought to be the most delicious of game birds; 19th-century gourmets considered thigh of woodcock to be the best bit. Allow one woodcock or two snipe per person. They should arrive with their insides intact (snipe will still have their heads on). This sounds unpleasant, but the insides are considered good eating, although you will have to remove the gizzard.

SERVES 4

4 woodcock or 8 snipe
4 slices of toast
unsalted butter
salt and freshly ground
    black pepper

Preheat the oven to 220°C, 425°F, Gas mark 7. With a small, sharp knife, make a small opening at the vent and insert your finger to remove the gizzard – it is a little round, hard lump, like a very thick button. Pull it out, cut it off and discard it. Push any of the trail (the insides) that came out with it back into the bird.

Should you wish your snipe to be presented *à l'ancienne*, skin the heads, turn them back to the body and use the long bills to skewer the thick part of the thigh, through the body, and out through the other thigh.

Place each bird on a slice of toast, season with a little salt and pepper, and roast in the hot oven, giving snipe about 10 minutes, and the slightly larger woodcock 15–20 minutes.

At the end of cooking, have ready very hot plates (or a hot serving dish). Remove the birds, lay the toasts on the hot plates, scoop out the remaining trail and mash with a little melted butter and seasoning; spread this over the toasts and place a bird on each one. This is not as unappetising as it may sound; the trail tastes like strong liver pâté.

Roast Pheasant with Pancetta and Lemon

SERVES 3–4

1 pheasant
1 lemon
75g (3oz) pancetta,
    thinly sliced
unsalted butter
1 teaspoon plain flour
150ml (5fl oz) stock made
    from the giblets of the
    bird, or from chicken
    or veal

Skin the pheasant (add the skin to the stockpot). Preheat the oven to 200°C, 400°F, Gas mark 6.

Peel the lemon by cutting off each end, then standing it on a board, and slicing off zest, skin and pith in vertical strips. Cut the lemon in the thinnest possible slices, removing any pips.

Lay the pheasant on its back and cover the breast and upper surface of the bird with the lemon slices. Then swaddle it up in pancetta, overlapping the slices where necessary. Take a piece of string, pass it under the back of the bird about halfway down the wings, then bring it up over the breast in a cross and back under in another cross somewhere near the middle of the thighs and finally up again, tying it neatly.

Lightly butter a roasting tin and put the pheasant in on its back. Roast, checking occasionally to make sure the pancetta isn't browning too much; if it is darkening a lot, turn the heat down slightly and roast for a little longer. After 20 minutes, reduce the heat to 180°C, 350°F, Gas mark 4 and roast for 20–30 minutes more. Test with a skewer pushed into the thickest part of the leg; if the juices run clear, or with only a hint of pink, it is done.

Remove the pheasant to a warmed serving dish and cut away the string. Pour the juices from the roasting tin into a small bowl and skim off the fat, returning about a dessertspoon to the tin. Sprinkle in the flour, then stir in the juices and mix to a paste. Add the stock, bit by bit, stirring constantly and bring to the boil; you should have a thin, well-flavoured gravy. Remove the pancetta (which should be crisp) just before carving, and serve.

Orange Sauce for Wild Duck

This is based on a recipe by Anne Cobbett in The English Housekeeper *(1840); it isn't clear which type of orange she used, but the bitter-sour flavour of Seville orange is better with this close-textured, gamey meat than sweet oranges, and makes a good midwinter combination. If you have to use sweet oranges, add a little bitter orange marmalade at the end, omitting the sugar. The 'bite' of the hot pepper is surprising, but very good with the duck. Roast the duck following the general method for game birds (see page 157). While the duck is roasting, make the sauce.*

SERVES 2

30g (1oz) unsalted butter

zest of 1 Seville orange, cut in
    fine strips and blanched in
    boiling water

a pinch of cayenne pepper,
    to taste

juice of 1 lemon

salt

sugar

Melt the butter in a small pan and add the orange zest, cayenne pepper and lemon juice. Bring to the boil and cook for a minute to reduce slightly. Taste, and add a pinch of salt and a little sugar until the bitter/sweet balance of the sauce is pleasing.

Salad of Game

A recipe inspired by Alexis Soyer, a famous chef in the 19th century, of salad leaves, game and sauce, producing a remarkably pretty, high Victorian result. The sauce should be made principally with cream; don't be tempted to turn it into a mayonnaise by replacing the cream with olive oil.

SERVES 4–6

a brace of roast grouse, or
    partridge, or a pheasant,
    cold
seasonal salad leaves

FOR THE SAUCE

1 medium egg yolk
1 small shallot, peeled and
    very finely chopped
1 teaspoon each finely chopped
    fresh parsley, tarragon
    and chervil
a small piece of fresh green
    chilli, finely chopped
1 tablespoon white wine vinegar
2 tablespoons mild olive oil
125ml (4fl oz) double cream
salt

FOR THE GARNISH

6–8 eggs, hard-boiled
unsalted butter, softened
2–3 anchovy fillets in oil,
    drained
1–2 gherkins, sliced
sprigs of chervil or tarragon

If you wish to serve this decorated in true 19th-century style, choose a shallow dish with a wide rim, and have a little softened butter ready. To make the sauce, put the egg yolk in a bowl and add the shallot, herbs, chilli and vinegar. Drizzle in the olive oil, stirring well. Season with salt. Whip the cream until very thick and stir into the mixture. Chill.

Carve the meat off the birds. Skin, trim and divide into neat pieces. Arrange the salad leaves on the serving dish and top with the meat. Pour on the sauce.

To make the garnish, peel the eggs and cut them in quarters lengthways. Arrange them around the rim of the dish, using a dab of softened butter under each piece to prevent it sliding around. Cut diamond shapes from the anchovy fillets and sliced gherkins, and use them to make a border round the edge. Add the herb sprigs as a final flourish.

GAME

165

Game Chips

These need maincrop potatoes, preferably ones that are long and quite regular in shape; Maris Piper are a variety that works reasonably well. It is difficult to recommend how many to use, as most people will eat as many game chips as you care to put in front of them, or until you get fed up with deep frying. You will also need oil or fat (beef dripping is best) for deep frying, and sea salt.

SERVES 2–3

Peel the potatoes and trim off any obviously irregular edges. Cut to give very narrow strips, about 2mm (1/16 in) thick and the same wide, and as long as the potatoes allow. Drop them into a bowl of cold water and leave to soak for about 15 minutes.

When you are ready to cook, drain them and spread on a cloth or kitchen paper and dry them thoroughly (this is important, otherwise they will make the hot oil spit viciously).

Heat the oil in a deep-fat fryer. The recommended temperature on a frying thermometer is 180–185°C (350–360°F). Alternatively, drop a small cube of bread into the hot fat and observe how long it takes to brown; if it rises to the surface and browns in 30 seconds, the fat is hot enough (don't let it get to smoking point, which is too hot).

When the fat is hot enough, fry the chips in batches – don't overcrowd the pan. Cook briskly until golden, then remove with a slotted spoon and drain well on kitchen paper.

Sprinkle with salt – a flaky one such as Maldon looks nice – and serve.

Salmi of Game

A salmi is a dish of game roasted very rare and allowed to cool, then reheated in a highly seasoned sauce. The recipe can also be used for reheating leftover game that has been roasted rare – although the result is really a hash. This dish became a classic of 19th- and 20th-century English game cookery.

SERVES 2–3

a brace of partridges or
    grouse or a pheasant
75g (3oz) ham
100g (4oz) onion, peeled
    and finely chopped
50g (2oz) carrot, finely
    chopped
15g (½oz) celery, finely
    chopped
1 teaspoon fresh thyme
1 teaspoon fresh marjoram
1 teaspoon fresh rosemary
½ teaspoon black pepper
¼ teaspoon salt
300ml (10fl oz) light stock
    or water
30g (1oz) unsalted butter
30g (1oz) plain flour
100g (4oz) button mushrooms,
    cooked in unsalted butter
1 tablespoon lemon or
    orange juice

TO SERVE
croutons or hot, crisp toast
lemon or orange quarters

Preheat the oven to 220°C, 425°F, Gas mark 7 and roast the birds for 10–15 minutes, or until nicely coloured. Remove and allow to cool. Cut off the breasts and legs, remove the skin and any fat, trim neatly, and put the meat in a cool place.

Put the skin and trimmings from the birds in a pan. Break up the bones and add them too, along with the ham, chopped vegetables, herbs, salt and pepper. Cover with the stock and simmer for 1 hour, adding a little more stock or water if the liquid seems to be evaporating too much. Then pour the contents through a sieve into a bowl. Press the debris in the sieve with the back of a wooden spoon to extract as much broth as possible, but don't rub any solids through (discard these).

Melt the butter in a clean pan and add the flour to make a roux. Allow it to cook gently for a few minutes until it turns a light brown. Then stir in the broth to make a smooth sauce. Taste, and add a little more salt if necessary. Add the mushrooms, lemon or orange juice and the pieces of game. Heat very gently – barely simmer – until the game is thoroughly hot.

Serve the game pieces in a warmed dish with the croutons or toast tucked round and the lemon or orange to garnish, and hand the sauce round separately.

Rabbit with Verjuice Gravy

A simple marinade using verjuice (see also page 38). It is a good flavouring for rabbit. If you can't get verjuice, use cider mixed with a little cider vinegar in this recipe. The rabbit can be stuffed with the mixture shown on page 174; if you wish to do this, add the stuffing after marinating.

SERVES 4

125ml (4fl oz) verjuice
3 tablespoons olive oil
freshly ground black pepper
1 rabbit
100g (4oz) unsmoked bacon
 or pancetta, thinly sliced
salt (optional)

Mix the verjuice, olive oil and a grind of pepper in a deep glass or china bowl. Put the rabbit into this mixture and let it marinate for 2–3 hours, turning occasionally.

Preheat the oven to 150°C, 300°F, Gas mark 2. When ready to cook, take the rabbit out of the marinade (reserve this) and wrap it in bacon. Place it in a roasting tin or dish in which it fits quite snugly and roast gently for about 1 hour. Then pour the marinade round it and continue to cook gently for another 30–45 minutes, by which time the meat should be cooked but not dried out. Keep an eye on it, and if the juices show signs of drying up and catching, add a little water.

Remove the rabbit to a warm serving dish. A relatively small amount of concentrated, nicely coloured juice should remain in the cooking dish. Make sure that you scrape any browned bits off the sides of the dish into the juices. Then skim off any excess fat, taste to check the seasoning (the bacon may have provided enough salt) and serve alongside the rabbit.

Two Sauces for Roast Rabbit

The first of these appears to have been a standard English accompaniment for roast rabbit in the 18th century. The second was quoted by Robert May, a chef writing in the late 17th century, as a list of flavourings, 'in the French fashion'.

Liver and Parsley Sauce

SERVES 4

the liver of the rabbit
1 small bunch of curly parsley,
    stems removed
50g (2oz) unsalted butter
salt

Simmer the rabbit liver very gently in a little water until it is just cooked – this will take only a few minutes. Drain, then chop finely.

Put the parsley in a small bowl and pour boiling water over it. Drain this and chop finely as well.

Melt the butter very gently and stir in the liver and parsley. Check the seasoning and add a little salt if necessary.

Onion and Mustard Sauce

SERVES 4

30g (1oz) unsalted butter
1 small–medium onion, peeled
    and finely sliced
1 dessertspoon Dijon mustard
lemon juice

Melt the butter in a small pan and cook the onion gently until translucent (don't let it brown). Stir in the mustard and thin the sauce with a little lemon juice.

Roast Rabbit with Apple

Rabbit responds well to the apple and cream treatment more usually associated with pheasant.

SERVES 4

3–4 tablespoons Calvados
    or whisky
1–2 tablespoons cider vinegar
the leaves from a few fresh
    thyme sprigs
4–5 juniper berries, crushed
1 rabbit
1–2 aromatic dessert apples
bacon fat, butter or olive oil
    for barding, optional
150ml (5fl oz) double cream
salt and pepper

Mix the Calvados or whisky, cider vinegar, thyme and juniper berries in a deep glass or china bowl. Put the rabbit into this mixture and let it marinate for 2–3 hours.

Preheat the oven to 150°C, 300°F, Gas mark 2.

When ready to cook, peel and core the apples and cut them into small chunks. Take the rabbit out of the marinade and stuff the body cavity with apples. Grease the roasting tin and put the rabbit in (bard the meat if desired, although this is not strictly necessary). Add the marinade, and cover with foil. Roast gently for about 1–1½ hours; check to make sure the juices don't catch, and add a little water or light stock if necessary.

When the rabbit is cooked, remove it to a warmed serving dish. There should be a small amount of concentrated juice left in the roasting tin (boil to reduce it to a few syrupy tablespoons if it seems on the liquid side). Add the cream and bring back to the boil; the sauce should be quite thick. Taste and adjust the seasoning.

Stuffing for Rabbit

Lemon and herb flavours are very typical of 18th- and 19th-century recipes for stuffing all sorts of meat. This is based on a recipe given by Anne Cobbett in The English Housekeeper *(1840).*

SERVES 4

50g (2oz) fresh white
    breadcrumbs
2–3 large fresh parsley sprigs,
    finely chopped
3 shallots, peeled and finely
    chopped
zest of ½ lemon (preferably
    unwaxed), grated
½ teaspoon salt
freshly grated nutmeg
freshly ground black pepper
1 medium egg yolk
about 2 tablespoons
    double cream

Mix the breadcrumbs, parsley, shallots, lemon zest and salt. Season generously with grated nutmeg and freshly ground pepper, then bind with the egg yolk and cream. Use this mixture to stuff the body of the rabbit, sewing the flaps of skin over to hold it.

Roast Hare

It is not strictly necessary to marinate a hare before roasting, but the meat does respond well to it.

SERVES 6

1 hare

FOR THE MARINADE

4 shallots, peeled and chopped

1 carrot, peeled, halved
   lengthways and cut
   in slices

1 bay leaf

4 tablespoons brandy

1 garlic clove, peeled
   and crushed

1 tablespoon roughly chopped
   fresh parsley

a few fresh thyme sprigs

a few black peppercorns,
   crushed

1 tablespoon olive oil

1 dessertspoon balsamic vinegar

Mix all the ingredients for the marinade together. Put the hare in a glass, pottery, plastic or stainless-steel bowl and pour over the marinade. Leave for at least 6 hours or up to 3 days, turning the meat occasionally in the mixture.

Remove the hare from the marinade, then stuff if desired (see recipe on page 177). Stitch the flaps together to hold the mixture and skewer the legs in place. Wrap the animal in bacon or pork fat and roast at 220°C, 425°F, Gas mark 7 for 15 minutes, then reduce the heat to 170°C, 325°F, Gas mark 3 and roast for another 40–60 minutes. Discard the juices from roasting, as they will contain the blood of the hare and curdle any gravy made with them.

Serve with Potatoes Roast in Cream and Herbs (see page 201) and redcurrant jelly.

Saddle of Hare with Cream Sauce

SERVES 2–3

1 saddle of hare
unsalted butter or olive oil
1 carrot, peeled
½ medium onion, peeled
1 garlic clove, peeled
salt
milk
200ml (7fl oz) beer
a little stock, preferably game
150ml (5fl oz) double cream

FOR LARDING
6 black peppercorns
2 cloves
the leaves from 2–3 fresh
    thyme sprigs
nutmeg
50g (2oz) pork back fat in a
    piece, or bacon rashers

For larding, grind the peppercorns and cloves to a powder with the thyme leaves. Grate in a little nutmeg and mix well. Cut the back fat into neat lardons, 3–4cm (1¼–1½in) long by 5mm (¼in). Roll in the spice mixture and use them to lard the saddle, drawing them into the meat at roughly 2cm (¾in) intervals, at right angles to the backbone. This can be done a few hours in advance.

Preheat the oven to 220°C, 425°F, Gas mark 7. When ready to cook, grease a small roasting tin lightly with butter or olive oil. Take the carrot and onion and cut them into rough chunks. Arrange them in the roasting tin, with the garlic clove, and sit the saddle on top, larded side up. Sprinkle with salt.

Put the hare in the oven and cook for 10 minutes. Baste a couple of times with a little milk. Then turn the heat down to 180°C, 350°F, Gas mark 4, and continue cooking for 15–20 minutes more. Halfway through this time, discard the milk and juices in the tin and pour over the beer. Baste again a couple of times.

When just cooked through (test by piercing the meat with a skewer; if the juices run clear or with just a hint of pink, it is done), remove the saddle to a warm serving dish and allow it to rest. Pour the cooking juices into a pan and skim off any fat. Add the cream and boil until only a few tablespoons remain. Taste and adjust the seasoning.

Stuffing for Roast Hare

This is enough for one hare (marinated first, if desired). See the recipe on page 175 for roasting instructions.

SERVES 4–6

125g (4½oz) slightly stale
    bread, torn into
    small pieces
½ small onion, peeled
    and finely chopped
the leaves stripped from
    6 fresh thyme sprigs
1 tablespoon finely chopped
    fresh parsley
2 anchovy fillets, chopped
    (if using salted ones,
    rinse well)
grated zest of ½ lemon
    (preferably unwaxed)
a generous pinch of nutmeg
a pinch of salt
freshly ground black pepper
stock or milk, to moisten
the pluck – heart, liver and
    kidneys of the hare
a little butter, for frying

Mix together all the ingredients except the stock and pluck, then use just enough of the liquid to moisten the mixture. Sauté the liver, kidneys and heart lightly in the butter, then chop and add to the stuffing mixture.

Haunch of Roe Deer Venison

A treat for a small dinner party. This recipe is based on one by the Scottish cookery writer Mrs Cleland, whose book A New and Easy Method of Cookery *was first published in 1755. It uses the old method of wrapping the joint before roasting. It is not strictly necessary to lard the meat, but it would be better to do so.*

SERVES 6

a leg of roe deer venison,
  1.5–2 kg (3½–4½lb)
100g (4oz) pork back fat, or
  fatty unsmoked bacon,
  cut into strips 5mm (¼in)
  by 3cm (1¼in)
salt and pepper
unsalted butter
4–6 tablespoons sloe gin (or
  use stock and 2–3 juniper
  berries)
1 tablespoon plain flour and
  1 tablespoon unsalted
  butter worked together
  to make a paste

Preheat the oven to 230°C, 450°F, Gas mark 8. Lard the meat with the back fat in neat rows (see page 15). Season with salt and pepper. Butter a large sheet of greaseproof paper, wrap the meat in it and tie with string like a parcel. Put on a rack in a roasting tin, and add a little water to the tin.

Roast for 20 minutes, then reduce the heat to 180°C, 350°F, Gas mark 4 and roast for another 1 hour. Some juice will drip through the paper into the tin. Add more water to the tin if the juices evaporate. Remove the paper and allow the venison to cook for a further 10 minutes. The juices should run fairly pink at this stage, but the meat should be just cooked through and not dry. Venison can be served quite pink if you like meat that way, so use your own judgement.

Put the venison on a hot plate to rest. Deglaze the roasting tin with the sloe gin or stock with juniper berries, and skim the fat from the surface. Put in a small pan and bring to the boil, then check the seasoning. Reduce the heat to barely simmering, drop in the butter and flour mixture in small pieces and stir through until it thickens.

Pot-Roast Shoulder of Venison

SERVES 6–8

about 100g (4oz) unsmoked
    bacon or pancetta in a
    thick slice
1 teaspoon black peppercorns
3 cloves
¼ nutmeg, grated
1kg (2¼lb) boned shoulder
    of venison
250ml (9fl oz) white wine
2 tablespoons verjuice
    (optional, see page 38)
4 fresh bay leaves, bruised
1 bouquet garni – fresh
    marjoram, thyme,
    rosemary, a slice of lemon
    and a few bruised juniper
    berries, tied in muslin
oil or dripping
2 medium carrots, scraped
    and cut into chunks
½ medium onion, peeled and
    cut into 4 chunks
¼ medium turnip, peeled and
    cut into chunks
15g (½oz) butter and 15g
    (½oz) plain flour worked
    together to a paste
1 tablespoon salted capers,
    rinsed and chopped
salt

Cut the bacon into lardons about 5mm (¼in) by 5mm (¼in). Grind the peppercorns and cloves together and mix with the nutmeg. Roll the lardons in the spices and use to lard the meat from the inside, stopping just short of the surface. Roll and tie the venison into a neat shape. Mix the white wine, verjuice and bay leaves in a large bowl and add the venison and bouquet garni. Leave for about 3 hours, turning from time to time.

Heat the oven to 140°C, 275°F, Gas mark 1. Heat a little oil in a flameproof casserole. When hot, add the carrots, onion and turnip, and fry until they begin to brown. Strain in the marinade and allow it to come to the boil. Add the venison and bouquet garni and cover. Put in the oven and cook for about 3 hours, turning occasionally.

By this time, the venison should be very tender. Remove to a warmed plate and discard the vegetables and bouquet garni. Boil the cooking juices fast until reduced to about half the original volume. Move the pan off the heat and drop in the butter and flour mixture in little bits, shaking the pan to mix it in. This should thicken the sauce a little. Add the capers, check the seasoning and add salt if necessary.

Serve, handing round redcurrant jelly along with the meat and sauce.

Best End of Red Deer Venison with Port and Redcurrant Jelly

A French-trimmed best end of red deer is an expensive joint, but is delicious and easy to cook. It is not essential to marinate this, but if doing so, leave for 2–3 days in the marinade. The sauce here recalls red wine sauces (port or claret) mixed with redcurrant jelly which were served in the 18th and 19th centuries, and the breadcrumb coating provides a pleasing contrast to the meat.

SERVES 4

1 best end of red deer
    venison, chined (backbone
    removed), the ends of the
    chop bones scraped bare
olive oil
salt
30g (1oz) dry breadcrumbs
30g (1oz) finely grated
    Parmesan
½ teaspoon allspice
freshly ground black pepper

FOR THE SAUCE
100ml (3½fl oz) port
3 tablespoons redcurrant jelly

Preheat the oven to 230°C, 450°F, Gas mark 8. Put 2–3 tablespoons olive oil in a roasting tin. Rub another 1 tablespoon oil into the meat. Salt it lightly and place, with the bones downwards, in the tin. Roast for 15–20 minutes.

While it cooks, combine the breadcrumbs, Parmesan, allspice and a generous grind of black pepper. Remove the meat from the oven, baste, and then pour the oil from the tin into the bowl with the crumbs. Mix well, adding a little more oil if it looks dry (it shouldn't be too oily, but there should be enough to help the crumbs cling together a little). Press the crumbs gently over the upper surface of the meat; some will fall into the tin, but try to avoid this as much as possible.

Turn the heat down to 180°C, 350°F, Gas mark 4, and roast for another 20–30 minutes, or until done to the point you prefer. Remove the joint to a hot plate and keep in a warm place.

To make the sauce, add the port to the roasting tin and stir with a wooden spoon to scrape up the cooking residues. Strain into a small pan and add the redcurrant jelly. Heat, stirring all the time to help the jelly melt, until simmering. Check for seasoning.

Carve by cutting down between each chop and serve on hot plates. Serve the sauce separately.

GAME

Poivrade Sauce

This was a classic accompaniment for venison in the late 19th and early 20th centuries. Recipes vary quite significantly in detail, but always aimed for a highly flavoured result. The consistent feature is a flavouring base of onions or shallots cooked in an acid medium, such as lemon juice or wine vinegar. Serve with a plainly roast joint.

SERVES 4–6

10–15g (¼–½oz) unsalted butter

30g (1oz) ham or unsmoked bacon, chopped

1–2 shallots, peeled and finely chopped

a piece of carrot 2–3cm (¾–1¼in) long, chopped

1 small slice of turnip, chopped

½ celery stick, chopped

a pinch of fresh thyme

1 fresh bay leaf

juice of 1 lemon

200ml (7fl oz) red wine

4 anchovy fillets, chopped

freshly ground black pepper

cayenne pepper

TO FINISH THE SAUCE

1 tablespoon unsalted butter

1 tablespoon plain flour

250ml (9fl oz) well-flavoured stock (beef for preference)

1 teaspoon redcurrant jelly or a pinch of sugar

Melt the butter in a saucepan and add the ham or bacon. Cook gently until the fat turns translucent. Add the shallots and other vegetables, then turn up the heat and fry briskly together, stirring frequently, until the vegetables begin to brown. Add the thyme, bay leaf and lemon juice, and allow the mixture to bubble until the liquid has reduced to almost nothing. Pour in the wine, add the anchovy fillets, a seasoning of black pepper and a pinch of cayenne. Cook gently for about 30 minutes, then rub through a sieve, discarding any debris.

To finish, melt the butter in a clean pan and stir in the flour to make a roux. Cook gently until the mixture turns a golden brown. Stir in the stock and bring to a simmer to thicken the mixture. Then add the red wine mixture and allow the sauce to cook very gently for about 30 minutes. Taste, add more seasoning if necessary (the anchovy will probably make it salty enough), and finish with the redcurrant jelly or sugar.

LEFTOVERS

Leftover bones from roast game make excellent stock (page 159), to use as the basis for soups and sauces. Sliced cold roast game bird meat makes excellent sandwiches. Venison from a prime cut can be delicious cold. Serve it with Cumberland sauce (page 194), and Watercress Salad (page 211). For reheating, Poivrade Sauce (opposite) is useful for making a hash.

GAME AND LENTIL SOUP

SERVES 4

2 tablespoons olive oil

100g (4oz) unsmoked bacon or pancetta,
    cut in 5mm (¼in) cubes

1 medium onion, peeled and chopped

1 garlic clove, peeled and crushed

½ a small celeriac, peeled and cut in
    5mm (¼in) cubes

2 small–medium potatoes, peeled and cut
    in 5mm (¼in) cubes

1 small sprig fresh rosemary

6 sprigs fresh thyme

100g (4oz) green lentils

1–1½ litres (1¾–2¾ pints) game stock (see page 159)

any leftover meat from the roast birds or scraps
    picked from the carcasses, cut into small pieces

salt and pepper

TO SERVE

fresh parsley, chopped

1 small garlic clove, peeled and chopped

breadcrumbs or croutons fried in unsalted butter

Heat the oil in a large saucepan. Add the bacon, onion and garlic. Cook briskly for a few minutes, stirring all the time, until the onion begins to turn golden. Add the celeriac, potatoes and herbs, and cook a little longer, then add the lentils and pour in the stock. Bring to the boil, add any meat scraps, and simmer gently for about 30 minutes. Check that the lentils are soft (cook a little longer if necessary). Taste and adjust the seasoning.

To serve, divide between 4 large bowls and top with a little parsley chopped together with garlic, or some breadcrumbs or croutons.

CROQUETTES OF GAME

A croquette should be small, dainty and, as the derivation of the word from the French croquant suggests, crunchy. They became a favourite 19th-century method for converting leftovers (of any meat) into something quite different through the medium of frying. It was a time when richness and elaboration in food were admired, and a substantial girth indicated wealth, and also plenty of servants to do the cooking. Serve with salad for lunch or as appetisers.

MAKES 16–18

180g (6oz) cold roast pheasant

50g (2oz) cooked ham, including some
    of the fat

2 medium mushrooms, sautéed in a little
    unsalted butter

10g (¼oz) unsalted butter

10g (¼oz) plain flour

150ml (5fl oz) stock

1 tablespoon medium sherry

a pinch of thyme

a squeeze of lemon juice

1 teaspoon redcurrant jelly

salt and pepper

oil or fat, for deep frying

FOR THE COATING

2 medium eggs

about 300g (10½oz) fine white breadcrumbs
    made from stale bread

Mince the game meat, ham and mushrooms together. Melt the butter in a small pan, stir in the flour, and make a sauce with the stock. Add the minced meat mixture, sherry and a little thyme. Cook over low heat for a few minutes, stirring well. The mixture should have the consistency of jam. Season to taste with a little lemon juice, redcurrant jelly, and salt and pepper. Pour the mixture into a shallow plate or onto a tray, and allow it to go completely cold.

Start the egg-and-breadcrumb process about 1 hour before you want to cook the croquettes. Beat the eggs in a soup dish or other shallow bowl. Put the breadcrumbs in another bowl.

Divide the cold meat mixture into portions, each the size of a small egg. Pass them through the beaten egg, then through the breadcrumbs, and leave for 30 minutes to dry. Repeat the process, and leave to dry for a little while.

Heat the oil in a deep-fat fryer to 175–180°C, 347–350°F. Deep-fry the croquettes until golden brown and thoroughly hot all the way through. Drain on kitchen paper and serve immediately.

HARE SAUCE FOR PAPPARDELLE

Leftover roast hare would have been hashed, just as most other meats were in British cookery, and presented with sippets of toast, croutons of fried bread, or possibly in a timbale of macaroni, the cooked pasta used to line a mould with the hashed meat as a filling. Today, the hare is more likely to be used for a pasta sauce in which the rich flavour of hare means a little goes a long way.

SERVES 4

olive oil

1–2 rashers unsmoked bacon, finely chopped

1 shallot, or ½ small onion, peeled and
    finely chopped

1 garlic clove, peeled and finely chopped

150g (5oz) cooked hare (not bits from the
    outside hardened by cooking, or
    sinew), minced

2 cloves, ground to powder

50ml (2fl oz) Marsala or Madeira wine

150–200ml (5–7fl oz) stock from the
    bones of the hare

chopped fresh parsley

salt and pepper

TO SERVE

about 450g (1lb) fresh pappardelle pasta

a little unsalted butter, melted

grated Parmesan

Heat a little oil in a frying pan and cook the bacon, shallot and garlic gently, stirring frequently, until the shallot begins to turn golden. Add the hare, the cloves and a grind of pepper. Pour in the Marsala or Madeira and let it boil away to almost nothing. Add the stock and parsley, and bring to the boil, then turn the heat down. Leave to simmer very gently for 1 hour (or more if you have time). Check occasionally to make sure there is some liquid left, but towards the end of the cooking time allow most of it to evaporate; this sauce should be fairly dry. Taste for seasoning and add a little salt if necessary.

To serve, stir into bowls of pappardelle that has been cooked, drained and dressed with a little butter. Serve with a bowl of grated Parmesan cheese.

VENISON PIES

For a relatively large amount of leftover venison, or to use untidy bits and pieces, mince the meat and use it in little pies – good picnic or finger food. They are nicest eaten just cooled on the day of making, but can be eaten hot from the oven or cold.

MAKES 18

200g (7oz) cooked venison
150ml (5fl oz) leftover gravy or
    Poivrade Sauce (page 182)
salt and pepper
shortcrust pastry made with 75g (3oz)
    fat and 150g (5oz) plain flour

Remove any fat and sinews from the venison and mince the meat fairly fine. Mix it with the gravy or sauce. Taste and add a little more seasoning if necessary, especially if the pies are to be eaten cold, as the flavour comes across more mildly then.

Preheat the oven to 190°C, 375°F, Gas mark 5. Roll the pastry out thin and stamp out 18 circles for the bottom crust of the pies. Use them to line patty tins and divide the venison mixture between them. Gather the pastry trimmings, re-roll and cut 18 slightly smaller circles for the tops. Cover and press down lightly to seal the edges.

Bake for 15 minutes, or until the pastry is golden brown.

Sauces,
Sides &
Vegetables

There are a plethora of sauces and side dishes in classic English cooking that are almost as essential to a roast dinner as the joint of meat itself.

From Bread Sauce (see page 190) to accompany poultry to Apple Sauce (see page 197), which goes perfectly with pork, many of our traditional sauces are intrinsic to the British culinary repertoire. There are also some sauces that might be less well known today, but are worth digging out of our historical cookery books – Cucumber Sauce (see page 193), for example, was popular with roast mutton in the 18th century and featured in John Thacker's *The Art of Cookery* (1758).

Mashed or roasted, the humble potato is a crucial element of the classic roast dinner. King Edwards are the quintessential potatoes for roasting, and they've been grown in the UK for over a century. As well as classic crispy roasties, potatoes can also be mashed until creamy or baked in a gratin, such as in the French-inspired Boulangère Potatoes (see page 199).

British culinary heritage has taken inspiration from all over the world when it comes to vegetables. They no longer have to take a back seat on the dinner plate, but can be transformed into impressive dishes that can take centre stage during the meal. With an increase in the number of people following vegetarian and vegan diets, as well as those who choose to simply reduce the amount of meat they consume, it is always a good idea to offer an array of vegetable options that are both interesting and substantial enough to create a meal in themselves.

Ragoo of Onions and Mushrooms (see page 209) is a delicious accompaniment to white meat, but made without the bacon and with a tasty vegetable stock, it's a lovely option for vegetarians. Sometimes just a small tweak is all that is needed to make a dish vegetarian-friendly: use butter instead of beet suet in Sage and Onion Stuffing (see page 198); use olive oil instead of dripping for Roast Potatoes (see page 202) and Roast Parsnips (see page 206); and use vegetable stock and vegetarian Parmesan in the Chestnut Gratin (see page 213).

Bread Sauce

A traditional accompaniment for roast poultry and game birds in English cookery. Recipes vary in the flavourings – nutmeg and mace appear in some, and onions are more usual than shallots. Be guided by personal taste and family tradition.

SERVES 4

300ml (10fl oz) full-cream
    milk
2 cloves
75g (3oz) shallots, peeled
75g (3oz) fine breadcrumbs
    made from slightly stale
    white bread
salt and pepper
3 tablespoons single cream

Put the milk in the top half of a double boiler or a bowl over simmering water. Stick the cloves into the shallots, add to the milk and leave to infuse for about 1 hour. Strain, discarding the shallots. Return the flavoured milk to the pan or bowl and stir in the breadcrumbs. Place over hot water again for about 10–15 minutes, during which the sauce should thicken up (not too much – if necessary add a little hot milk). Taste and add a little salt and pepper. Stir in the cream and serve.

A Sauce for Cold Meat

The original of this was given as 'A sauce for Partridge, or Moor Game' in the pompously named Culina Famulatrix Medicinæ *published by Ignotus (otherwise known as Dr A. Hunter) in 1807. It produces a surprisingly modern result, and is also delicious with roast meat.*

SERVES 4

4 salted anchovies, well rinsed
2 fat garlic cloves, peeled
juice of ½ lemon (you may not
    need all this)
180ml (6fl oz) olive oil
freshly ground black pepper
cold roast meat, cut in small,
    neat pieces

Put the anchovies, garlic, half the lemon juice and the oil in a blender and whizz together. Taste, and add more lemon juice if you wish; you might also like to add some pepper, although it is unlikely that any salt will be needed.

Mix with the roast meat. Serve this on a bed of salad leaves or with lightly cooked French beans, or broccoli spears, or small new potatoes.

Red Onion 'Marmalade'

A simple take on a modern classic, to eat warm with plain roast duck.

SERVES 4

30g (1oz) unsalted butter
1 red onion, peeled, cut in
    half and sliced thinly
1 tablespoon sweet sherry
2 tablespoons red
    wine vinegar
a piece of star anise
20g (¾oz) light soft
    brown sugar
salt and pepper

Melt the butter in a small heavy frying pan. Add the onion, cover and cook very gently for about 30 minutes, stirring occasionally. It should become soft and translucent, but not brown.

Add the sherry and let it bubble a moment, then add the wine vinegar and a piece of star anise and bring the mixture to the boil. Stir in the sugar, season with a little salt and pepper, and simmer gently, stirring frequently, for 15–20 minutes more, or until it has achieved the consistency of runny jam. Remove the star anise before serving. Serve freshly made as an accompaniment to roast duck.

Cucumber Sauce

Cooked cucumber was popular in the 18th century, and was often served with roast mutton. The original recipe, 'To make a Salpicon for Roast Meats, as Beef, Mutton, Veal or Lamb', was recorded by John Thacker in The Art of Cookery (1758). A salpicon is a mixture of chopped ingredients bound in a thick sauce, then used as a garnish or stuffing; make it a little more liquid and it becomes a sauce. It also works as a vehicle for leftover meat. Do use good stock to make this. Thacker suggests, 'You may add Sweetbreads, Morels, Trufles, Lamb-stones [testicles] and Pallets, Coxcombs, Mushrooms, or any of these that you can get.'

½ cucumber, peeled, the seeds removed and the flesh cut into 5mm (¼in) dice
½ small onion, peeled and finely chopped
250ml (9fl oz) red wine vinegar
30g (1oz) unsalted butter
a little ham or lean unsmoked bacon, finely chopped (optional)
2 tablespoons plain flour
250ml (9fl oz) good meaty stock or gravy
salt and pepper

Put the cucumber, onion and vinegar in a small bowl and leave to soak for 1 hour. Drain, discarding the vinegar, and blot the vegetables dry on kitchen paper.

Melt the butter in a frying pan. Add the ham or bacon and allow to brown a little. Then add the onion and cucumber and cook briskly until they are starting to brown slightly. Stir in the flour, then gradually add the stock, stirring to produce a sauce about the thickness of double cream. Taste, add salt and pepper, and serve with plain roast lamb or mutton.

If making this with leftovers, any gravy left from the roast can be used in place of part of the stock. Add the leftover meat, sliced, right at the end and allow it to heat through gently (if the sauce becomes very thick, add a little more stock, or water if nothing else is available).

Cumberland Sauce

A delicious sauce for cold ham or game. It appears to have no links with the county of that name, and a legend associating it with the royal title of the Duke of Cumberland appears to be just that – a legend. The base of redcurrant jelly and wine is reminiscent of 18th-century sauces for venison, but the first recognisable recipe was given (under a different name) by Alexis Soyer in 1853. It seems to have been the French chef Georges Auguste Escoffier who popularised the recipe and made it a commercial success in the 19th century.

SERVES 4–6

zest of 1 orange (preferably
    unwaxed), cut in
    thin strips
zest of 1 lemon (preferably
    unwaxed), cut in
    thin strips
4 tablespoons redcurrant jelly
4 tablespoons port
1 teaspoon smooth
    Dijon mustard
a pinch of ground ginger

Put the orange and lemon zest in a small bowl, then cover with boiling water and leave to blanch for 3–4 minutes. Drain well.

Melt the jelly in a small pan, stirring to smooth out any lumps. Add the port and mix well. Stir in the zest, the mustard and a little ginger. Taste and add a little more mustard or ginger if desired. Allow to cool before serving with cold meat.

Apple Sauce

Apple sauce is a traditional accompaniment for pork and goose. It is very simple to make: peel and core 2 large Bramley apples, then cut into small pieces. Cook gently in a small pan with just enough water to prevent them from sticking. Stir frequently. Once they have become a purée, add about 3 teaspoons of sugar, or to taste.

Caramelised Apples

These are good served with pork, goose or duck. If serving with duck, add a little grated orange zest at the end. The apples must be a firm-fleshed type that will keep their shape when cooked.

SERVES 4–6

30g (1oz) unsalted butter
3 large apples (Cox's or a
    dryish, aromatic eating
    apple), peeled, cored and
    sliced, but not too thinly
a piece of star anise (optional)
1 dessertspoon cider vinegar
2 tablespoons sugar

Melt the butter in a heavy frying pan and add the apple slices, and the star anise if using. Cook gently, stirring frequently, until the apple is softening and has become slightly transparent. Add the cider vinegar, then the sugar and continue to cook until the apple begins to caramelise. Serve tepid.

Sage and Onion Stuffing

This recipe – suitable for pork, goose or duck – was considered old-fashioned by the 1840s. It was also thought too overpowering by Victorian cooks, although Eliza Acton remarked that some people always liked it with leg of pork (which was stuffed at the knuckle end). It has outlived Victorians and remains one of the most iconic mixtures in the English kitchen.

In her otherwise excellent recipe on which the one below is based, Mrs Roundell in Mrs Roundell's Practical Cookery Book *(1898), suggested that a very few well-blanched sage leaves were sufficient. We are accustomed to much bigger flavours, so I have added a few more and omitted the blanching. A mixture based on one onion is about the right amount for stuffing a duck; double it for a goose.*

SERVES 4–6

1 large onion, peeled
12 fresh sage leaves, washed
60g (2½oz) stale breadcrumbs
20g (¾oz) unsalted butter,
    cut in small pieces (or
    beef suet for a traditional
    mixture)
1 medium egg, beaten
½ teaspoon salt
a little freshly ground
    black pepper

Put the onion in a pan, cover with boiling water and simmer for 20–30 minutes, or until tender. Drain. Once it is cool enough to handle, cut it into quarters. Put it in a food processor with the sage and chop (but don't reduce it to a purée), or chop together by hand until fairly fine. Stir in the breadcrumbs, butter and enough egg to bind lightly, then stir in the seasoning (don't use the processor, which makes the mixture too runny).

Use to stuff a boned and rolled pork roast or a bird, or press into a greased dish and bake along with the roast for the last 30 minutes of cooking time.

Boulangère Potatoes

A dish of French origin, popularised in Britain during the love affair with French food in the mid-20th century. Marcel Boulestin gave an early version in his book Simple French Cooking for English Homes *(1930). It is similar to* tiesen nionod, *a Welsh dish of onions and potatoes baked together like a gratin.*

SERVES 4–6

2 large onions, peeled and
    thinly sliced
unsalted butter, for frying
    and for greasing the dish
about 750g (1lb 10oz) baking
    potatoes, peeled
150ml (5fl oz) well-flavoured
    stock
salt and pepper

Preheat the oven to 180–190°C, 350–375°F, Gas mark 4–5. Fry the onions gently in butter to soften them, but don't let them colour (they can be blanched in boiling water if you prefer). Slice the potatoes thinly.

Grease a shallow ovenproof dish with butter and arrange the potatoes and onions in layers, seasoning well as you go. Finish with a neat layer of overlapping potato slices. Dot with butter and pour in the stock; it should come almost to the top of the dish.

Bake in the oven until the potatoes are soft and the surface nicely browned. A little extra (hot) stock or water can be added during cooking if the dish seems to be drying out, but this dish is better for not swimming in liquid.

Mashed Potatoes

I can't remember where I first came across this version, but I think it was in a 19th-century book and the writer stated that it was the way the French made mashed potato.

SERVES 4

500g (1lb 2oz) potatoes
30g (1oz) unsalted butter
salt and pepper

Peel the potatoes, then cut into chunks and boil as usual. When tender, do not pour the cooking water down the sink, but drain it into a jug.

Add the butter to the potatoes and season with salt and pepper. Mash the potatoes, adding a little of the reserved cooking water and continuing to mash, adding more cooking water if necessary, or butter if you want, until you feel they have achieved the right consistency.

Potatoes Roast in Cream and Herbs

This is not a traditional method for roasting potatoes, but it is good with just about any meat, especially game.

SERVES 4–6

2–3 fresh rosemary sprigs
    about 6cm (2½in) long
8–10 fresh sage leaves
12 fresh thyme sprigs
1–2 garlic cloves, peeled
750g (1lb 10oz) potatoes,
    peeled and cut in 2cm
    (¾in) chunks
200ml (7fl oz) double cream
1 teaspoon salt
freshly ground black pepper

Preheat the oven to 200°C, 400°F, Gas mark 6.

Strip the leaves off the rosemary and chop them together with the sage, thyme and garlic. Mix the potatoes, cream, chopped herb mixture, salt and some pepper. Put them in an ovenproof dish or small roasting tin that holds them comfortably in a shallow layer.

Cook for about 30 minutes, stirring once or twice. By the end of this time, they should be tender (give them a little longer if not), and the cream should be thick, clinging to the potatoes, and lightly flecked with gold on the surface.

Roast Potatoes

Roast potatoes are a defining element of 'a proper roast'. King Edward, a potato variety with almost iconic status in Britain, probably has the best flavour, and can develop a fantastic crisp crust and melting interior. Wilja and Desirée are also good; Cara and Romano should produce reasonable results.

SERVES 4–6

1kg (2¼lb) potatoes
about 50g (2oz) fat for
    roasting, such as beef
    or pork dripping
salt

The oven needs to be hot – 200–220°C, 400–425°F, Gas mark 6–7. Peel the potatoes. Leave small ones whole, and cut large ones into smaller pieces (3–4 each). Put them in a pan, just cover with cold water, and bring to the boil. Boil for 5–7 minutes. Tip them into a colander and drain well.

Put the fat in a roasting tin and place in the oven to melt and get very hot. Take it out and add the potatoes. (Wear oven gloves and an apron in case the fat spits – it should be hot enough to sizzle satisfactorily.) Turn the potatoes well in the hot fat, sprinkle with salt, and roast for 40–50 minutes. In a gas oven, put the potatoes at the top. Turn once or twice during cooking, and add a little more salt each time.

Cabbage

SERVES 4

1 pointed cabbage or
    Savoy cabbage
about 15g (½oz) unsalted
    butter, bacon fat or
    olive oil
a few juniper berries, bruised
1–2 tablespoons cider vinegar
salt

Trim the cabbage leaves of their central stalk, wash and shred the leaves. Put them in a pan with a well-fitting lid. The water clinging to the leaves after washing should be enough, or add 2–3 tablespoons. Add the butter, juniper berries and a little salt. Put the lid on the pan and put it on the lowest heat for about 15 minutes. Look occasionally to make sure that the cabbage isn't drying up; add a small amount of water if it is. When just tender, add the cider vinegar, mix well and serve.

Red Cabbage

SERVES 6

1 generous tablespoon goose,
    pork or bacon fat, or oil
1 medium onion
1–2 apples, preferably sourish
    ones
1 small red cabbage
2–3 tablespoons cider vinegar
2 tablespoons light pale
    brown sugar
4–5 cloves, bruised
5cm (2in) cinnamon stick
1 piece of orange zest
    (preferably unwaxed)
    about 5 x 2cm (2 x 1in)
1 teaspoon salt
freshly ground black pepper

Preheat the oven to 140°C, 275°F, Gas mark 1. Peel and roughly chop the onion. Peel, core and chop the apples. Quarter the cabbage, discard the stem and finely slice.

Heat the fat in an ovenproof casserole and fry the onion until translucent. Stir in the apples, then the cabbage, and fry lightly for a few minutes. Add the other ingredients and stir well. Cover and transfer to the oven for about 1½ hours. This can be cooked on the hob, but the heat must be very low – and stir frequently, adding a little more water from time to time if it shows signs of drying up.

Roast Parsnips

This is a root that goes well with roast beef. Parsnips are considered to be at their best in winter, after the first frosts – freezing temperatures convert some of the starch in the living roots into sugar, and this caramelises when they are cooked. Look for ones that are fresh and firm; flabby parsnips don't cook well.

SERVES 4–6

about 500g (1–1½lb) parsnips
about 50g (2oz) fat for
    roasting, such as dripping
    from beef or pork, or lard
salt

The method for cooking these is similar to that for Roast Potatoes (see page 202). Wash and trim the parsnips and scrape off the skin with a peeler. Cut, on the diagonal, into slices about 5mm (¼in) thick. They can be parboiled for about 5 minutes, but if they are good and fresh, this isn't necessary. Put the fat in a roasting tin in a hot oven at 220°C, 425°F, Gas mark 7.

Drain the parsnips well if parboiled, then tip into the hot fat (protect your hands with oven gloves). Turn them around in the fat, sprinkle with a little salt, and roast for 10 minutes. Turn the heat down to 190°C, 375°F, Gas mark 5, and cook for another 20–30 minutes, stirring occasionally so that they develop nicely browned surfaces. Drain well before serving.

Ragoo of Onions and Mushrooms

'Ragoo' was the 18th-century English cook's phonetic rendition of the French ragoût. Complex mixtures requiring two or three different meaty stocks, these dishes were all the rage at the time. They were used as sauces and garnishes, or could be dishes in their own right. This one is good with white meat poultry of all sorts – and can also be served with beef, mutton or game. A good meaty stock based on chicken or veal, plus some ham, bacon or gammon, is essential.

SERVES 4

2 tablespoons olive oil
1 small onion, peeled and
 very finely chopped
1 celery stick, trimmed and
 very finely chopped
1 medium carrot, trimmed
 and very finely chopped
100g (4oz) lean unsmoked
 bacon or gammon, very
 finely chopped
400ml (14fl oz) well-flavoured
 stock
a bouquet garni of fresh
 parsley, thyme, marjoram
 (optional)
400g (14oz) shallots or very
 small onions, peeled
200g (7oz) button
 mushrooms, trimmed
salt and pepper

Heat the oil in a saucepan. Add the onion, celery and carrot and fry briskly, stirring frequently until the vegetables begin to caramelise and turn golden brown at the edges. Add the bacon and continue to fry for another 5–10 minutes. Any trimmings from the mushrooms can be added too. Pour in the stock, then add the bouquet garni. Once the mixture has come to the boil, turn it to the lowest possible simmer and leave to cook until reduced by about half.

Put the shallots and mushrooms in a clean pan. Strain the reduced stock over them, pressing so that all the flavoursome juices pass through (but don't rub any of the solids through). Continue to cook very gently, stirring from time to time. By the time the onions are tender (about 45 minutes), the stock should be reduced to a few spoonfuls of thick, slightly syrupy liquid, just coating the vegetables. Taste and adjust the seasoning.

Crisp Fried Browned Onions

Useful as a garnish for all sorts of leftover meat and potato dishes, and good in cold beef sandwiches (see page 210). It may take a couple of goes to master this, but it's worth the effort.

SERVES 2–4

sunflower oil, for frying
1 large onion, peeled, halved
    lengthways and sliced
    very thinly

Line a plate or small tray with a few sheets of kitchen paper. Heat a layer of oil about 1cm (½in) deep in a frying pan (a heavy cast-iron one is best). Add the onions and regulate the heat so that they cook fairly fast. Partially cover the pan, so that there is a small gap for steam to escape. You will need to remove the lid and stir them fairly frequently, to make sure they cook evenly. Don't let them brown patchily.

When the onions start to look shrunken and are beginning to brown, leave the lid off and stir constantly. They should begin to brown quite rapidly; at this point, watch them closely. You want them to be brown, not burned. When they begin to change colour to a deeper, caramel brown, turn off the heat and remove them immediately with a slotted spoon. Scatter them over the kitchen paper to absorb any remaining oil.

Watercress Salad

A salad of watercress has a long history of accompanying roast birds at table. Served with duck, it usually had orange segments added, but if pomegranates are available, I think they are better.

SERVES 4

2 bunches of watercress,
    washed and picked over
the seeds of ½ pomegranate
    (or use the segments of 2
    oranges – cut off the pith
    with a small, sharp knife)

FOR THE DRESSING
scant 1 teaspoon smooth
    Dijon mustard
1 tablespoon wine vinegar
salt and pepper
4–5 tablespoons olive oil

For the dressing, mix the mustard and vinegar together, then season to taste. Stir in the oil.

Toss the watercress with the dressing, then scatter with the pomegranate or orange and serve at once.

Puréed Brussels Sprouts

During the early 1980s, it seemed that all vegetables had to be served as purées, a fashion derived from the then influential French nouvelle cuisine. They have mostly had their moment and gone, but Brussels sprouts are good done this way and go very well with game birds.

SERVES 4

500g (1lb 2oz) Brussels
    sprouts, trimmed
125ml (4fl oz) single cream
salt and pepper

Cook the sprouts in boiling water until tender. Drain well. Process with the cream and add seasoning to taste. Don't overdo the processing – you should be left with a beautiful pale-green purée, lightly flecked with darker green, like a piece of jade.

Chestnut Gratin

An accompaniment to game birds that is also good for turkey. Peeling chestnuts is tedious, but the results are lighter and fresher-tasting than using tinned purée.

SERVES 4–6

600g (1¼lb) chestnuts in
    their shells
300ml (10fl oz) stock
    (appropriate to the roast),
    or chicken stock or milk
30g (1oz) unsalted butter
salt
3 tablespoons dry
    breadcrumbs
3 tablespoons grated
    Parmesan cheese

Cut a slit in the shell of each chestnut and cook them in boiling water for about 15 minutes. Take off the heat, remove them from the water a few at a time, and when just cool enough to handle, peel off the brown outer shells and the inner membrane. Return the shelled chestnuts to a clean pan and cover with the stock. Simmer gently until very tender, then pass the whole lot through a sieve to make a purée.

Preheat the oven to 200°C, 400°F, Gas mark 6.

Beat the butter into the chestnuts, add a pinch of salt, and pour into a buttered gratin dish. Mix the breadcrumbs with the Parmesan and scatter over the top. Brown in the oven for about 15 minutes.

Conversions

Weights

7.5g	¼oz
15g	½oz
20g	¾oz
30g	1oz
35g	1¼oz
40g	1½oz
50g	1¾oz
55g	2oz
60g	2¼oz
70g	2½oz
80g	2¾oz
85g	3oz
90g	3¼oz
100g	3½oz
115g	4oz
125g	4½oz
140g	5oz
150g	5½oz
170g	6oz
185g	6½oz
200g	7oz
225g	8oz
250g	9oz
285g	10oz
300g	10½oz
310g	11oz
340g	12oz
370g	13oz
400g	14oz
425g	15oz
450g	1lb
500g	1lb 2oz
565g	1¼ lb
680g	1½ lb
700g	1lb 9oz
750g	1lb 10oz
800g	1¾ lb
900g	2lb
1kg	2lb 3oz
1.1kg	2lb 7oz
1.4kg	3lb
1.5kg	3½lb
1.8kg	4lb
2kg	4½lb
2.3kg	5lb
2.7kg	6lb
3.1kg	7lb
3.6kg	8lb
4.5kg	10lb

Volume

5ml	1 teaspoon	
10ml	1 dessertspoon	
15ml	1 tablespoon	
30ml	1fl oz	
40ml	1½fl oz	
55ml	2fl oz	
70ml	2½fl oz	
85ml	3fl oz	
100ml	3½ fl oz	
120ml	4fl oz	
130ml	4½fl oz	
150ml	5fl oz	
170ml	6fl oz	
185ml	6½fl oz	
200ml	7fl oz	
225ml	8fl oz	
250ml	9fl oz	
270ml	9½fl oz	
285ml	10fl oz	½ pint
300ml	10½fl oz	
345ml	12fl oz	
400ml	14fl oz	
425ml	15fl oz	¾ pint
450ml	16fl oz	
465ml	16½fl oz	
500ml	18fl oz	
565ml	20fl oz	1 pint
700ml	25fl oz	1¼ pints
750ml	26fl oz	
850ml	30fl oz	1½ pints
1 litre	35fl oz	1¾ pints
1.2 litres	38½fl oz	2 pints
1.5 litres	53fl oz	2½ pints
2 litres	70fl oz	3½ pints

All eggs are medium unless stated otherwise. Use either metric or imperial measures, not a mixture of the two.

Length

5mm	¼in
1cm	½in
2cm	¾in
2.5cm	1in
6cm	2½in
7cm	2¾in
7.5cm	3in
9cm	3½in
10cm	4in
18cm	7in
20cm	8in
22cm	8½in
23cm	9in
25cm	10in
28cm	11in
30cm	12in
35cm	14in
38cm	15in

Oven Temperatures

Description	Fan	Conventional	Gas
Very cool	100°C	110°C/225°F	Gas ¼
Very cool	120°C	130°C/250°F	Gas ½
Cool	130°C	140°C/275°F	Gas 1
Slow	140°C	150°C/300°F	Gas 2
Moderately slow	150°C	160°C/320°F	Gas 3
Moderately slow	160°C	170°C/325°F	Gas 3
Moderate	170°C	180°C/350°F	Gas 4
Moderately hot	180°C	190°C/375°F	Gas 5
Hot	190°C	200°C/400°F	Gas 6
Very hot	200°C	220°C/425°F	Gas 7
Very hot	220°C	230°C/450°F	Gas 8
Hottest	230°C	240°C/475°F	Gas 9

Index

Further Reading

Acton, Eliza, *Modern Cookery for Private Families*, 1855 edition with an introduction by Elizabeth Ray (Southover Press, 1993)

Beeton, Isabella, *Beeton's Book of Household Management*, 1861 edition (Chancellor Press, London, 1982)

Bradley, Martha, *The British Housewife*, 1756 edition with an introduction by Gilly Lehmann (Prospect Books, 1996)

Cobbett, Anne, *The English Housekeeper* (1840)

Davidson, Alan, *The Oxford Companion to Food* (Oxford University Press, 1999)

Dickson Wright, Clarissa, and Johnny Scott, *Sunday Roast* (Kyle Cathie, 2006)

Edington, Sarah, *Complete Traditional Recipe Book* (National Trust Books, 2006)

Fearnley-Whittingstall, Hugh, *The River Cottage Meat Book* (Hodder and Stoughton, 2004)

Kenney-Herbert, Colonel, *Common-Sense Cookery* (Edward Arnold, 1905)

Luke, Harry, *The Tenth Muse*, revised edition edited by Peter and Michael Luke (The Rubicon Press, 1992)

Paston-Williams, Sara, *Good Old-Fashioned Jams, Preserves and Chutneys* (National Trust Books, 2008)

Rogers, Ben, *Beef and Liberty* (Chatto and Windus, 2003)

Thacker, John, *The Art of Cookery*, 1758 edition with an introduction by Ivan Day (Southover Press, 2004)